IN THE
SHADOW
OF A
MOUNTAIN

A SOLDIER'S STRUGGLE WITH
POSTTRAUMATIC STRESS DISORDER

Susan Dahlgren Daigneault

SUSAN DAHLGREN
DAIGNEAULT

IN THE SHADOW OF A MOUNTAIN

Copyright © 2012, by Susan Dahlgren Daigneault.
Cover Copyright © 2012 by Sunbury Press, Inc.

For information about special discounts for bulk purchases, please contact Sunbury Press, Inc. Wholesale Dept. at (717) 254-7274 or orders@sunburypress.com.

To request one of our authors for speaking engagements or book signings, please contact Sunbury Press, Inc. Publicity Dept. at publicity@sunburypress.com.

FIRST SUNBURY PRESS EDITION
Printed in the United States of America
November 2012

Trade Paperback ISBN: 978-1-62006-149-7
Mobipocket format (Kindle) ISBN: 978-1- 62006-150-3
ePub format (Nook) ISBN: 978-1-62006-151-0

Published by:
Sunbury Press
Mechanicsburg, PA
www.sunburypress.com

Mechanicsburg, Pennsylvania   USA

Foreword

Many ordinary men and women who came from "the greatest generation ever" served without protest in the US armed forces during World War II. Many of these folks came home from this conflict suffering with what we now call PTSD (Post-Traumatic Stress Disorder) and, without protest or complaint suffered in silence for 40-50 years. These men and women experienced emotional turmoil when remembering their experiences...nightmares, vivid memories and flashbacks...emotional isolation and numbing... bouts of depression...anxiety and irritability... feelings of dread...problems with concentration... poor sleep. Ed Dahlgren, who I had the pleasure of meeting late in his life and hopefully helped some to relieve his suffering, was one of these people. Despite being heroic enough to merit receiving the Congressional Medal of Honor, Ed suffered for years in silence and "soldiered on" in his life (holding a job and raising a family despite his ongoing distress). I think it is a great thing that his daughter (with support and encouragement from all of his family) has elected to share Ed's story. Hopefully others who have suffered in silence will be encouraged to step forward and receive the assistance they need when they discover that even a true war hero was not immune to psychiatric problems and was willing to seek assistance. It is possible that Ed Dahlgren's most heroic acts came long after his military service.

Stuart Wyckoff, MD

Presque Isle, Maine

La Montagna

The picture postcard beauty of the Italian hills in
summer is now but a distant memory, replaced by
the daily reality of cold and sleet, foxholes full of
mud when they can be dug. Soldiers' boots slip on
the wet boulders, which sometimes cut the leather
and let in the muck. And then there's the noise,
indescribable and never-ending noise. Nebelwerfer
fire from a six-barreled rocket mortar raining down
in volleys of six, machine gun rat-a-tat, solitary
bullets from snipers hiding high up on the
mountain whiz by and, more often than not, find
flesh. And then the screams. "I'm hit. Help me!
Help me! I can't feel my legs!" Or worse, the thump
of a body hitting the ground followed by silence.

On the morning of February 11, 1944, a blinding
snowstorm blows in, adding to the misery of the
bitter cold and freezing uniforms made wet by the
sleet of yesterday. Despite the brutal conditions, the
soldiers of the Texas 36th Infantry Division keep
moving inch by inch up the rocky slopes of Monte
Cassino which is crowned by a 1,400-year-old
Benedictine Abbey. The Germans are using the
slopes of the Abbey as an artillery observation point;
overwhelming machine gun fire from these slopes
picks off American soldiers just like at a shooting
arcade on Coney Island. Unlike the Germans who
hold the high ground and have had three months to
sow mines and booby-traps into the ravines and
gullies of the mountains, the Americans have no
natural shelter as they attempt to reach the enemy.

Despite the wretched conditions, a young soldier
keeps moving forward, mindful of his directive to
seize and hold Hill 468. Crawling slowly, his face
just inches from the frozen Italian soil, he cradles
his rifle in both hands, using his elbows to propel
himself. He knows snow and cold weather; these
conditions bring back memories of winters growing

up in Northern Maine. Snow feels and smells the same no matter where it comes down, on enemy territory or not.

Night falls over them, but the noise of combat continues. If he lifts his head just a few inches, he can see the lights of the monastery at the top of the mountain, the house of God that the Nazis now hold. He wonders about the Nazis' concept of God, if they have one, given the seemingly god-forsaken situation that the enemy causes him to be in. And he thinks about whether or not he'll survive this day. Earlier in his tour, he'd wondered how he'd be in combat, would he freeze up or run or go crazy. Now with several months of service behind him, he knows he's okay, that he's able to handle the fear that comes with the job. Today, every day, he focuses on the job that he is here to do.

Someone beside him screams. "I'm hit! Help me!" His instinct is to help so he stands up, trying to ascertain where his fellow solder has fallen. As he listens for another "help me," he is knocked to the ground. A piercing pain spreads out all across his shoulder. He must have taken a bullet. He runs a hand up the front of his jacket but doesn't feel any blood. He concludes that the bullet hasn't gone completely through his body; it must be lodged somewhere in his back. He lies still, trying to pick out sounds close by as opposed to the familiar background noise of the battle.

He hears German voices, likely a patrol sent out to finish off any wounded enemy soldiers. The injured soldier nearby calls another, more feeble "help me." A shot rings through the darkness, and there is no more calling out. Lying still as a corpse, the wounded soldier knows that his possible survival rests on his ability to not take a breath, not move a muscle. The German voices come close. "Was ist hier? Tot oder nicht?" A boot kicks his leg, but he doesn't flinch. "Tot." Dead to the Germans, he's escaped a second bullet.

He stays completely still through the cold February night, afraid that he might freeze to death on the side of this mountain, knowing that this is his only option if he wants to live. It is the longest night of his life. Fortunately, the cold staunches the blood lost from his shoulder wound, but the cold can't dull the pain which provides him with a focal point throughout the night. He can't remember having ever felt anything like this. He's never broken a bone or had any illness more serious than scarlet fever. His mind turns to memories of growing up in northern Maine with his sister and cousins, and for the first time in such a long time, he thinks of his mother, Minnie. He has tried to curb any memory of those days in order to focus on the present situation, but tonight he allows himself to remember. He recalls skipping school to go fishing with a friend and being forgiven for his antics by Minnie. He remembers the times when Minnie was happy and how her blue eyes would sparkle in the sun when she laughed. He thinks about how he wasn't there with her at the end. He remembers her, his Minnie, dead now since June and wonders if he is soon to join her.

And sometime during the night, as he muses about happier times, the noise lets up. Even Germans must sleep, he thinks. But he doesn't sleep, too afraid of moving in his sleep and attracting the attention of a rogue sniper quietly moving along the rocky slope.

As the sky lightens, signaling the new day, he tries moving slightly, just to see if he can. His shoulder throbs. The pain is intense but, yes, apparently he can still move. He hasn't frozen to death, which permits hope, hope that he might possibly get out of this situation. He crawls for a while on his belly, listening intently for enemy voices, again holding his rifle in his arms. It seems that he's been crawling for hours. He passes no other living soul but sees many dead soldiers lying face down in the snow, dead he knows because of entrails curling out from abdomens, from enormous wounds above the eyes.

As he moves along, the shadow of the mountain is replaced by a cold sun, letting him see the terrain more clearly. Sometime during the night, the snow stopped, but the cold still prevails. He can see that the enemy isn't close by. Gambling on his safety, he stands up. His right arm is limp. He carries his rifle in his left arm.

He finds a mule trail, the sole means of supplying American soldiers with ammo and rations. The trail is empty today and makes for easier walking. The trail winds around boulders and gullies. He walks slowly, carefully listening and watching for anything that could spell danger.

Just when it seems that he can't walk another inch, he sees an American convoy passing close by. He waves his one good arm, trying to attract the attention of just one of the soldiers walking beside the armored vehicles. "Over here. Look here!" A soldier looks up and seeing that the voice belongs to a fellow Yank, he runs over. "What happened to you?" the soldier questions him. Too relieved and too much in pain to reply, he falls to the ground. "We need a stretcher! This man is hurt."

Introduction

The soldier who walks down a mule trail off from Monte Cassino in the early morning hours of February 12, 1944, with a German bullet lodged in his right shoulder will survive and fight many more battles before his war ends with the surrender of the Germans in May of 1945. The story of his war reads like the newsreels of the era that precedes the main feature at the movie houses: Salerno, the Rapido River, the Rhone Campaign, winter in the Vosges Mountains, the Siegfried Line. He will be in the front lines for weeks at a time without a break. At one low point in his experience, his company of fifty men will decline to only seven. As the platoon sergeant, he is told to go down the line of fresh replacements and select forty men he wants to go with him, knowing as he points to that one and then the next that he could well be sealing their fate. He will try his hardest, as he has for all of the men who fight with him, to take no unnecessary chances and to always go first when the command comes to move forward. Despite his care and caring, many of his men will die, outnumbered and out of luck. He could easily have died with them but doesn't, and throughout his long life he wonders why his life is spared and questions how he will be able to live with the memories of the experiences of killing and being killed.

When the war ends, this soldier returns home a highly decorated hero who will be honored by the president who bestows on him the Congressional Medal of Honor in a ceremony in the East Room of the White House on August 23, 1945. He and twenty-seven other heroes, all with visible and hidden scars, are all equally humble about receiving this award, cognizant of the many other heroes with whom they served who also deserved this honor but who would not be returning home. Despite the decorations, the ribbons, the medals, he will return home and will seldom talk about his war experiences, seeking not opportunities to share stories with old friends, preferring the comfort of a warm fire and a good book. Over time, the physical wound will heal, but the deeper, more troubling emotional wounds will not go away. This emotional suffering, known today as posttraumatic stress, and its companion, survivor guilt, color the rest of his life.

This soldier, clever at keeping the emotional toll private, tries to carve out a life worthy of his survival. He suffers from flashbacks, stutters and stammers on the telephone, chain smokes, and sometimes stares out the kitchen window—looking for what? searching for what?—lost to his family. He works sixty-hour weeks to provide for his growing family, walking miles upon miles each day despite the frequent and bitter pain of kidney stones. He and his wife join the PTA and go to their children's events. He is active in the American Legion and enjoys, to a certain extent, the camaraderie that is to be had with other veterans.

He is one of the original group of citizens who join together to improve recreational opportunities for the young people in the community. He becomes known in the community as an honest man, a hard-working man, a family man, a man of integrity. He has many friends, most who know nothing about his war experiences because he chooses not to talk about the past.

As is often the case with PTSD, his grows worse as time passes and climaxes after his retirement when he has more time on his hands. He turns to religion as a way to find peace, becoming a devout Catholic and a leader in the parish. Still, the ghosts of the past haunt him.

He has the courage to seek treatment, not always what men of his era would do. Medication and therapy help and over time bring a measure of peace. And....bring our beloved father back to us.

The soldier in this story is my father, Edward C. Dahlgren. I have written his story for many reasons, among them the simple fact that writing about him helps me to deal with his death. As I write his story, according to my memories of him, I suffer his absence but also keep him close. When I recall growing up with Dad, riding in the car with him or tossing a softball back and forth on the front lawn, I see him still with the unfiltered Camel cigarette hanging from the side of his mouth, the small side window on the driver's side of the car open a crack so the smoke can go that way and not bother me.

These memories prompt smiles and a warm feeling. And I want others to know about this love story, about this father who had no father of his own, but who knew how to be the very best of fathers. And I want to tell the story of how a soldier who endures horrifying battlefield experiences and returns home to fight a lifetime of posttraumatic stress and survivor guilt, creates a life worthy of his survival. I want his legacy of public service and goodness to be remembered.

I want readers to understand that the war experiences of our soldiers often do not end when the guns fall silent. Physical wounds may heal but as combat veterans age, the incidence of PTSD rises. Dad had the courage to seek help for his PTSD, and I tell his story so that others will follow his lead and seek treatment. No one should suffer in silence when resources are available to ease the pain.

I've heard it said that we need to study history so that we don't commit the mistakes of the past. Our current situation, with American soldiers fighting on two fronts in Iraq and Afghanistan, would suggest that we have not studied history closely enough. Many soldiers are returning from their war experiences with horrific wounds, both physical and emotional. They will need our nation's financial support for many decades to come, and we must not be frugal when it comes to providing for their needs. I write this book to bring attention to this most important issue.

As I learned first-hand when I visited Oberhoffen, France, in August 2009, there is no such thing as a "good war." War devastates communities and families for generations, particularly so if the battlefields happen to be in your own backyard, as was the case in Oberhoffen. The people of Oberhoffen still revere Dad these many years later and consider him a consummate hero for his efforts on a street named Winter to rid the village of its German occupiers. In order to be "saved" from German occupation, ninety percent of the village of Oberhoffen was destroyed. Apart from the long ago Civil War, we Americans do not know the cost of war fought on our own turf. Those of us alive today cannot fully know the pain of war, but as I learned in Oberhoffen, Charles Walther and Madam Wagner and Charles Christmann know. I want to tell some of their stories as well, so that we will know better the cost of war.

Although this book belongs to Dad and might be dedicated to him, I dedicate it to all the soldiers who have fought for our freedom, especially the many who didn't come home and those whose heroic acts went unwitnessed and therefore were not honored with our nation's awards. Dad would have liked this.

Lt. Edward C. Dahlgren, Medal of Honor recipient, decorated on August 23, 1945 in Washington, D.C.

"What you have experienced, no power on earth can take from you."

--Viktor Frankl

...nearly all men are afraid, and they don't even know what causes their fear—shadows, perplexities, dangers without names or numbers, fear of a faceless death. But if you can bring yourself to face not shadows but real death, then you need never be afraid again, at least not in the same way you were before."

—John Steinbeck, East of Eden

Chapter One

The Hidden Costs of War:
Posttraumatic Stress Disorder

"Combat was hell and I have many terrible memories of death and destruction. But the memories of total camaraderie with the men who shared that hell will forever be embedded in my heart.

I'm not proud of some of the things that happened during my combat. It comes back to haunt you. When I got back, I had a hard time sleeping. I was very nervous. I had dreams, not pleasant dreams.

But I did what I thought had to be done. I did a lot of damage, let's say it that way, to the Germans.

You have a certain objective and you try to save as many of your men's lives as possible. You don't know what you're doing at the time. You're frightened, you know, later, but you just have to keep going and not show your fear.

I don't consider myself a hero. Having the Medal of Honor for me is about doing a good job, what you're supposed to do: duty and sacrifice.

I wouldn't do it again. I don't think so now. I don't think it is morally right to kill people. I've thought of this for the past three or four years. I can sympathize with the conscientious objectors in our country."

—Edward C. Dahlgren

What was known as shell shock in World War I and battle fatigue in World War II would be given another name in 1980 when the American Psychiatric Association added Posttraumatic Stress Disorder to the third edition of its Diagnostic and Statistical Manual of Mental Disorders. From that point to the present, PTSD is recognized in psychiatric circles and in everyday life as a powerful force that can stay with a veteran for all of his post- war life.

PTSD affects its victims in many ways: intrusive and distressing recollections of the trauma, debilitating flashbacks, horrific nightmares, sleep difficulties,

1

irritability, hypervigilance, feelings of detachment or estrangement from others, emotional numbing (for example, the inability to have loving feelings), the sense of a foreshortened future, guilt, anxiety, depression, and withdrawal or estrangement from family. (Reid & Wise, 1995). Time diminishes the intensity of traumatic memories, but the wounds never quite seem to close.

Nearly every combat veteran who saw other soldiers killed carries around the survivor's mantra: 'Why him, why not me?'" (Gelman, 1994). While busy raising families and carving out a career, these veterans may suffer in silence but appear to function quite well on the surface; but as they retire and lose the daily structure that served them well for years, many of these old soldiers are re-experiencing the war and are becoming re-traumatized. One researcher describes "a waxing and waning of difficulties over the forty-year postwar experience" (Zeis & Dickman, 1989, 80), with PTSD symptoms resurfacing in force as these veterans age. Other researchers find that World War II veterans exposed to heavy combat have 13.3 times greater risk for the return of PTSD symptoms 45 years after the war as compared to noncombat veterans (Spiro, Schnurr & Aldwin, 1994).

Born in an era when men stoically suppressed their feelings and kept a proverbial stiff upper lip, World War II veterans have either not sought psychological interventions or delayed seeking such help for decades. Recent research on PTSD suggests that this stoicism has dire consequences and links PTSD to coronary heart disease (Kubansky, Koenen, Spiro, Vokonas & Sparrow, 2007), gastrointestinal problems, and joint pain (Elder, Shanahan & Clipp, 1997; Schnurr & Spiro, 1999). Some studies indicate that veterans who have experienced horrific combat experiences are twice as likely as the general population to develop cardiovascular disease, diabetes, ulcers, high blood pressure, and cancer later in life (MacKenzie, 2005). They are also prone to self-medicating: alcohol during the day and sleeping medication at night help to temporarily put the demons to rest. Veterans Administration surveys estimate that 210,000 survivors of World War II, now in their eighties and beyond, continue to suffer symptoms of PTSD (MacKenzie, 2005).

In addition, researchers have found a link between alexithymic behavior—a difficulty describing feelings in words, (Elder et al, 1997) and physical decline. It is as if "physical symptoms provide the outlet for the psychic discomfort" (Elder et al, 1997, 336). The link between PTSD and physical decline with aging is so pronounced that a study conducted by Lee et al. found that 56% of World War II veterans who experienced heavy combat are chronically ill or dead by age sixty-five (Lee, Vaillant, Torrey & Elder, 1995).

These studies describe my father's experience with PTSD. Like most other World War II veterans, he kept his psychic pain to himself, suffering in silence for over 50 years. He never talked about his war, except for those occasions when reporters requested interviews, and being the polite man that he was, he would sit and answer questions, questions that focused on the facts of his war and not on the affective impact of those battles upon his very soul.

I was nine before I had any inkling of the meaning of the many medals he kept tucked away in a dresser drawer. My siblings and I knew of those medals but instinctively, we knew not to ask Dad for the stories that went with the medals. When he marched in Memorial Day parades, we'd watch him, busting with pride, completely unaware that he was one of our country's most highly decorated veterans. To us, he was simply Dad in his Legion cap, marching with his buddies on a day set aside to remember our loved ones, especially our soldiers who died for their country.

Before the 1980's and the naming of the collection of symptoms now known as PTSD, we had no way of knowing the source of various behaviors that we noticed in Dad. We knew that Dad had tremendous difficulty talking on the phone or making conversation with strangers; he stuttered and stumbled over words, and it was painful to watch him and listen to him as he tried to get the words out. I also remember his nervous habit of tapping out a cadence with his fingers when he sat at the kitchen table: One, two, three, four. One, two, three, four, five. On and on went the tapping, the expression on his face telling us that he was lost in another place. Where did you go, Dad, when you left us in this way?

Although he couldn't tell us about his war, we were always aware of his physical pain. He suffered terribly from kidney stones, likely not a souvenir from the war but a malady passed on to him from his mother. For one long winter, he spent several months hospitalized at the Veteran's Hospital in Togus, Maine, where doctors attempted to find something that would help him with the kidney stones. Nothing seemed to give him relief from the all too frequent agony of these events. He developed diverticulitis, a painful intestinal condition. Before he reached 62, he would experience congestive heart failure which forced him into early retirement and meant that the small bottle of nitroglycerin tablets would reside in perpetuity on a kitchen shelf, to be tucked into his pocket whenever he left the house. Diabetes would enter his life in his 70's.

Until I was 12, Dad drank with his veteran buddies over card games on many Friday nights. On some of those nights, he wouldn't make it home until the next day, when my mother would light into him, dumping any remnants from a mostly consumed fifth of whiskey down the kitchen sink. She did not allow alcohol in her house and completely disapproved of his drinking binges. A car accident when he'd been drinking and an ultimatum from Mom lead to him giving up alcohol for good. Smoking, though, was another matter. It would take a heart attack to scare him into quitting cold turkey.

As the years went on, his stuttering diminished. He was busy with work and with raising a family of four. I believe sheer willpower kept many of the debilitating symptoms of PTSD in check. Only in retrospect can I now understand that even during this time, he was wrestling with soulful questions. In the 1970's, he started instruction in the Catholic Church and became a devout attendee at Sunday Mass. Research indicates that this interest in finding solace in religion is common among victims of PTSD whose deep psychological wounds damage the very soul of the soldier (Tick, 2005). Despite the comfort that his involvement in the Church gave him, religion didn't cure.

With retirement, the issues came back in full force. The flashbacks came back, along with intrusive thoughts. He grew increasingly anxious and depressed, to a point where Mom suspected he might take his own life. He started abusing over the counter and prescription sleep and pain medications. He isolated himself from all of us, staying in bed for most of the day. When his requests for prescriptions for pain and sleep medication increased, his doctor and my mother convinced him to see a psychiatrist. He went reluctantly, but over time, therapy and the right medications provided him with a certain measure of peace.

However, the damage had been done. Years of sleep and pain medications, likely taken more often than recommended, would lead to internal bleeding and eventual death. It was as if the war, in the end, killed him.

Before he left us, he showed us how one person can rise above personal challenges and contribute meaningfully to both his family and his community. Although Dad always questioned why he had been spared death on the battlefields in Italy and France, I know in my heart why he survived: he had work to do back home. Although he was decorated in war with many medals for courage above and beyond the call of duty, it was the valiant way in which he faced the demons of PTSD and the example he left us of how to live a life full of meaning that provide a lasting illustration of what it is to be a hero.

Chapter Two

The Pre-War Years: Precursors to PTSD

"If you're looking for a helping hand, look on both ends of your arms. You've got two."
– Almina "Minnie" Anderson Dahlgren

That my father remembers his mother's injunction about hard work long after her death is a key to how he defines himself as a self-sufficient, hardworking man who will do what has to be done because it is his duty. As her only son whose father died tragically before he was born, Edward learns early, long before his childhood ends, that his mother depends on him to be a man. To that end, he quits high school when he turns sixteen, finds work and turns his pay envelopes over to her. And when he goes off to war, once again he is duty-bound to do his best. And when his best isn't good enough and when he can't keep his men alive and safe, he suffers. And, like the stoic Swedes who raised him, he doesn't express his pain but instead goes on with the work of each day.

That his experiences growing up in Northern Maine, the son of a young widow, would contribute to his predisposition for developing PTSD after his war ends is supported by research on the topic of risk factors predicting PTSD (Brewin, Andrews, & Valentine, 2000). Several of the predictive factors identified in a meta-analysis, including general childhood adversity, lack of education, and previous trauma (Brewin et al, 2000, 748) are all a part of my father's early years. His father died even before he was born, and his mother was not able to keep their farm going. For room and board for herself and her two young children, she would become an unpaid housekeeper for her brother-in-law. In his early years, Dad would always have enough to eat because of the potato fields encircling his uncle's home, but he wouldn't have such luxuries as trips to the dentist to take care of decaying teeth or a new bicycle. And because of the restrained nature of his Swedish relatives, he would not know praise or physical examples of love. A capable student who was advanced two grades in elementary school so that he could start high school with his older sister, he was too small, too shy, and eventually too sick to enjoy school. He left school at the end of his sophomore year. In later life, his lack of education would trouble him.

And, what could it have been like for a young man to unexpectedly lose his mother, his sole parent, to cancer just prior to his involvement in the ferocious battles that would mark his next two years? With no time to mourn and no family to console him, his feelings were simply put away, boxed up, and never examined, except on the rare occasion between battles when he would allow himself a moment to remember. With no one to really come home to, what did it matter if he took risks during combat? In the end, the only thing that would matter was his fellow soldiers, and he fought hard to keep them safe.

What follows is the story of Dad's early years, the years that formed his character and   factored greatly in how he was able to survive a war that was one horrendous battle after another.

The Swedes of Northern Maine

Lured to Northern Maine with the promise of land, the first Swedish immigrants arrive on Saturday, July 23, 1870. Though the State of Maine had promised them twenty-five completed log cabins and cleared land when they get there, the Swedes find only six of the twenty-five cabins ready for them. Used to hard work and cold, these Swedes set to clearing the land and building more cabins. By late fall, other Swedes arrive, increasing the size of the new colony to 114. They continue to build houses, clear land, and construct a large public building that serves as church, school, and meeting house.

By the mid-1870s, there are 1300 Swedish immigrants living in Maine, most of whom populate the Northern

Maine communities of New Sweden, Stockholm, Woodland, Jemtland, Perham, and Colby Siding. The communities thrive on the sale of potatoes and wood products and the expansion of the Bangor and Aroostook Railroad to the area leads to even greater economic growth. One-room school houses, churches, stores, rooming houses, a shingle mill, a saw mill, and a starch mill all crop up in the various communities. By all accounts, this is a good time and a good place to be alive. With extended families close by and neighbors who share their heritage, the members of the community feel a certain pride of place, happy with raising families who will become first generation Swedish-Americans.

The first Dahlgren to arrive in Northern Maine is Gustaf who, with his brother Carl, left Skelleftea, a coastal town close to the Arctic Circle in Sweden, early in 1875. The brothers land in Gloucester, Massachusetts, where Gustaf will meet his future wife, Ida. They marry in July of that year. While brother Carl decides to strike out for the American west, Gustaf and Ida head to Northern Maine where land is promised for the price of clearing it and the building of a dwelling.

Gustaf and Ida settle on one hundred acres in Perham, Maine and join with the other hardworking Swedes in clearing land, building homes, and planting crops such as potatoes and buckwheat. The land is rich, and the Swedes prosper from their efforts. Gustaf will later buy 83 more acres, paid for with the buckwheat that he grows on the land, land that can be passed along to his sons as they grow into adulthood. On November 26, 1876, their first son is born. They name him Edward Carl Gustaf for the twin brother who went west, for another brother who stayed in Sweden, and per tradition, for his own father. Over the years, seven more sons and a daughter will complete the family.

As the oldest son, Edward receives the first parcel of land from his father, a 25-acre section adjacent to his parents' farm. With cleared land, a house, and a bright future ahead of him, Edward is ready to take a wife and chooses the lovely Almina Anderson, known as Minnie, who lives on a prosperous neighboring farm. The year is 1910.

The young couple speak Swedish to each other in the privacy of their home and practice their English in Caribou where they go for supplies once a month. By all accounts they are happy together, enjoying the simplicity and structure of farm life with its predictable seasonal chores and bounty from hard work. Their happiness will expand with the birth of their first child, Ruth Alverne, in 1913. Like their parents before them, they hope for many more healthy children in the years to come.

Tragedy Strikes

Almina weeps, quietly and privately. It is not acceptable to show emotions publicly, even in such a situation as hers. Stoicism is a virtue among her people. Can that stoicism, though, have contributed to the situation she now finds herself in? If only husband Edward had mentioned the pain earlier, would he now be alive? What use is it now to look back? Edward is just now dead, dead in their bed from a ruptured appendix. The doctor arrives too late to save him and can only pronounce the cause of death.

It is October, 1915. In the Swedish settlements of far Northern Maine, nature shows off her colors, her final hurrah before the bitter cold and blowing snows of winter. The harvest is soon to end, potatoes safely stored in barns for winter sales. Edward is intent on getting all of his crops out of the field. He isn't going to let the pain in his side keep him from his work. At the time of his death, there are still potatoes in the ground.

"What will we do now? " Almina asks herself. A young widow with a three-year-old who suspects a new life will be coming in the spring, she cannot do the men's work to keep the farm going.

She needn't worry yet. Her brothers and Edward's brothers come with their horses and equipment and finish the harvest. They stack wood for the stoves, bring water in from the well, and sometimes take a break to sit at the kitchen table with Almina and take a glass of coffee. She enjoys the company.

By December, she knows that she is in fact pregnant, just as she had suspected back in October when Edward died. Daughter Ruth will have a sibling to care for; a new one will perhaps ease the loneliness of the long winter nights and days. Still, despite the help from her family, Minnie worries about how she will be able to provide for her young family. Although the farm sustains them, there is nothing extra to put aside for a rainy day. If she can't plant a crop in the spring, then she will not be able to stay on the farm.

As the winter progresses, Almina looks out over the snow-covered fields, hoping to see Edward coming in from the barn. Of course, that will not happen but still, she hopes. And she hopes that the new life soon to arrive will be healthy and that she will be brave and quiet during the birthing.

On March 14, 1916, Almina's latter wish comes to be. In the bed in which she lost her husband in October, Almina gives birth to a healthy boy. She names him for his father: Edward Carl Dahlgren. And for as long as she lives, she will provide for him as best she can. She silently makes this pledge to her newborn son as she rocks him gently in the wicker rocker that had been a gift from husband Edward when their first child arrived. She rocks and strokes her baby's head, softly humming a Swedish song.

Later in the spring, Almina's brothers talk with her about the farm. A single woman with two young children and no money to hire help would not be able to work the farm. They propose a solution. Her youngest brother, Ernest, wants to farm but has no land. Ernest will plant crops on Almina's farm and over time, with profit from the crops, will gradually pay her for the land and buildings. The farmhouse with its huge appetite for wood and water is much too much for Almina alone. Brother Albert's store has a small apartment upstairs, a space that will be much more convenient for Almina and the children. The heat from the woodstove in the store will mean fewer trips to the woodpile for Almina and food for the children is just a staircase below them. It is agreed that this is the best plan.

Almina and the children will live above the store—until another tragedy strikes.

An Arrangement

Almina has two sisters, Ida and Davida. The pretty Ida catches the eye of John Dahlgren, one of Edward's younger brothers. The two marry and have two children, Clifford and Viola. Viola is the same age as Almina's daughter Ruth. When Viola is just a toddler, her mother dies from complications due to diabetes. John, a carpenter, asks his mother, Ida Dahlgren, to care for Viola. John has a home that he built but no one in the home to care for a young child.

Grandmother Ida Dahlgren is happy to care for her granddaughter. Over time, she realizes that perhaps the two tragedies that befell the Dahlgrens can be turned into a positive outcome. A widow with no home and two children and a widower with a home but no housekeeper might be able to forge an arrangement that can work for both families. Uncle John will work and support the household in exchange for Almina caring for the children and taking care of the housework. This is not to be a marriage, merely an arrangement that suits both families.

Once again, young Edward moves, this time to the home of his Uncle John, the place that he will call 'home' until he returns from military service.

Eddie is the youngest of the four children under Uncle John's roof. Slight with dark brown hair that falls into his blue eyes despite Minnie's lick and a promise to try to keep it back, Eddie is all ears and nose, features that he'll have to grow into. A tease from the beginning, young Eddie loves teasing the girls. A quick pinch on an arm invokes a "Minnie, Eddie pinched me." Minnie's "Now, Eddie, stop that," will fall on deaf ears.

Taciturn and undemonstrative, Uncle John leaves Minnie in charge of discipline and gives Eddie over to his brothers and brothers-in-law for instructions on how to

11

fish, hunt, and tend to the horses. Uncles take him fishing. He quickly learns where the best fishing holes are located and how to reel in the brook trout that are plentiful. Other uncles teach him to fire a rifle. A natural "good shot," these early lessons will later make the difference when hitting a target can mean his survival...or not. Eddie loves spending time on the farms of his extended family. A favorite place to be is the barns and a favorite pastime is combing the horses, giving Minnie yet another reason to scold. "Eddie, you smell like the barn and I bet you've brought in more fleas. What am I going to do with you?"

If he isn't in the barns or down at the brook, Eddie can be found across the street at Grammie Ida's house, content in her ample kitchen, soaking her warm, soft molasses cookies in his glass of farm-fresh milk. Eddie is a frequent visitor and a welcome one who keeps her loneliness at bay for a while. With all of her children grown and husband Gustaf dead from the diphtheria that also took their son, Allen, Ida enjoys the mischievous Eddie who is not above sneaking some extra cookies into his trouser pockets so that he'll have a little something additional for the evening.

I was just twelve years old when I started high school in Caribou after six years at the one room school house in Woodland. I was just a little fellow and bashful. Living out in the country, I couldn't participate in things. I didn't enjoy high school a bit in this world and left at sixteen. It wasn't anybody's fault. It just happened that way.

Becoming a Man

Fortunately for Minnie, school gives her a respite from her youngest. An able scholar who is advanced by two grades and enters high school at the same time as his older sister Ruth and cousin Viola, Eddie is a quick study in arithmetic and recess games. He is an able athlete and especially loves playing baseball in the dirt yard of the school house. Ever the imp, he is not above taking a day off from school when spring fishing looks favorable.

The house that John built is just a short distance from the railroad spur that provides the local children a train ride into Caribou to attend high school. Eddie is merely thirteen when he enters the ninth grade at Caribou High School. Small for his age, he is much smaller than the other students in his class. Too small for basketball and dependent on the train schedule to get back home, Eddie finds high school is not as enjoyable as the time he spent at the little consolidated school back home. During his third year of high school, he comes down with scarlet fever and misses an entire term. He never goes back, convincing Minnie and Uncle John that he can work and bring money into the family, a far better option than finishing high school.

The Depression is in full swing, but rural communities such as those in Northern Maine are not as affected by the economic crisis as more urban centers. Families have their farms which produce enough food for the community. Wood for heat is plentiful. Crops have to be planted and harvested despite the economic woes of the country, and Eddie, like the other men in the area, is always able to find work on the farms, in the sawmills, or with the State crews that are building roads in Northern Maine. Despite his small stature and relative youth, he gains a reputation as a hard worker, reliable and strong. There is always work available for those such as Eddie who will give an employer 110% effort for a day's pay. Even when dog-tired after a long day lifting heavy potato sacks and moving them from one section of the storage barn to another, he thinks of Minnie and her advice. "If you're looking for a helping hand, look on both ends of your arms. You've got two."

He continues to live in the house with Minnie and John, turning over his pay every week for his keep, holding onto just enough to be able to enjoy a trip into Caribou to see a movie or have some change to gamble away at a poker game with one of his friends. Life is relatively good for Eddie during the 1930s with work plentiful, friends always available, and the baseball leagues in need of players with talent. During this time, he gains a considerable reputation as a standout baseball player, a catcher, playing in the leagues that sprout up in towns across Northern Maine. He has a strong arm and a sharp eye which means his bat seldom misses a strike over home plate.

"Even though Dad did not enjoy his high school years, one thing he did enjoy about that time in his life was going to the dances and shaking a leg with the ladies. Several years ago, he told me the story about a friend of his from Colby Siding who will be identified as 'Everett'. It seems there was a big school dance scheduled for the upcoming weekend and practically all of the boys in the area were really looking forward to attending. Unfortunately, Everett was, like many young people of that time, in dire need of dental care that simply was either unavailable or unaffordable. Everett wound up having to have all of his teeth extracted and was fitted for a set of inexpensive dentures which would not arrive in time for the big dance. He really wanted to go to that dance. Not wishing to see him miss the gala event, Everett's mother let him borrow her dentures and away he went to the dance with Dad and the other fellows. According to Dad, his mother's dentures were at least half again a size too big for poor Everett and made him resemble nothing else as much as the neighbor's old draft horse down the road, but Everett was at the dance, and he was dancing with the young ladies, and all was right with the world."

Michael J. Dahlgren

Leaving Maine, 1942

Over time, Eddie's cousins and sister marry and move out of Uncle John's house. Eddie continues to live at home, but as the 1930s wind down and talk of war begins, young men start to leave the area's farms and mills for the nation's industrial centers. Work in what will become the war industries is becoming plentiful, with jobs reputedly paying better than those in Northern Maine. As his friends leave for Worcester, Massachusetts, Eddie feels the urge to join them. Although saddened to think of her youngest leaving, Minnie knows that Eddie has to make his own way in the world.

Eddie leaves Northern Maine after the potato harvest in the late fall of 1941, heading for the machine shops of Worcester where many of his friends have already gone and found steady work. Not long after he leaves home, Minnie moves to Portland to live with her married daughter.

Eddie rooms with friends from Maine who work at the same machine shop. Life in Worcester with its movie theaters, baseball games, and dance halls appeals to this crowd of young singles who for the first time in their lives have extra change jingling in their pockets.

As the war progresses and the military's need for young recruits grows, life for young single men is facing change. Eddie's roommates gradually leave to enlist in the military, giving up their draft deferments for working in the defense industry. He knows that he will be joining them soon. In early 1943, when his draft notice comes, he decides not to seek another deferment but sign up, joining his friends in the war that is now raging all over the globe.

Before heading for Fort Devens to enlist, he wants to see his mother. He has just enough time to catch a bus to Portland to see his mother and sister. It is a poignant visit for Minnie who suspects that this will be the last time she will see her son, not because of her fears for his well-being, but because of the knowledge she has of her own ill health, information she doesn't share with her son.

Decades later, Eddie will still remember this last goodbye to his mother Minnie. *"I can see her now, standing on the top of the stairs, crying. I can hear her tell me, 'Take care, dear. I love you.' She was a good woman, a good mother."*

Alabama in 1943

Returning to Massachusetts from his visit with his mother, Eddie reports to Fort Devens for induction into the service. A Marine Corps recruiter looks him over, thinking this young man would make a good new prospect, but changes his mind when he learns that his teeth are in bad shape.

Eddie enlists in the Army and is sent to hot, humid, unfamiliar Alabama for training. Assigned to a unit full of Texans, the 36th Infantry Division, he feels the outsider that he is. He works hard and his skill at shooting, learned through years of experience in the Northern Maine woods, gains him some respect from his new acquaintances.

"Where you from, soldier? You sure talk funny."

"Maine."

"Maine? Where's that?"

"North."

"Never heard of it. How far north.?"

"A long ways from here. New England. Gets cold there."

"Well. I guess we're stuck with you. Funny way of talking and all. One thing you're going to need to know about us Texans—we're really proud of being Texan and when we hear the song, 'The Yellow Rose of Texas,' we drop what we're doing, take off our hats, and put a hand over our hearts. We'll expect that you'll be doing this, too."

"Doesn't sound like too much to ask. Guess I can do that."

The laconic man from Maine and the Texans get along just fine. Not only does Eddie join his fellow soldiers in their way of honoring their home state, he also impresses them with his marksmanship and poker skills. They like him and when he is given opportunities for leadership, they follow him willingly, trusting him on some deep, instinctive level that he will take good care of them.

The Yellow Rose of Texas

Oh, the yellow rose of Texas is the only girl I love.
Her eyes are even bluer than Texas skies above.
Her heart's as big as Texas, and wherever I may go,
I'll remember her forever because I love her so.

There are so many roses that bloom along the way,
But my heart's in Amarillo and that's where it will stay
With the yellow rose of Texas, so I'd better get there fast

'Cause I know I was her first love and I want to be her last.

Oh the yellow rose of Texas is the only girl I love.
    Her eyes are even bluer than Texas skies above.
Her heart's as big as Texas, and wherever I may go,
    I'll remember her forever because I love her so.

Saying Goodbye, June, 1943

April passes into May, which gives way to June. On a day in mid-June, Eddie Dahlgren is called to his commanding officer's quarters. "Son, I hate to tell you this but we just received a telegram from your sister up in Portland. She says that your mother passed last night and that they would like you to try to get north for the funeral."

"Are you sure you have the right person? My mother hasn't been sick."

"You're Edward Dahlgren, correct?"

"Yes."

"And your sister's name is Ruth Riley?"

"Yes."

"Then, I'm sorry to say that this news does belong to you. Now, we can give you a few days leave, so you'd better get going."

He makes a collect call to Ruth. "Ruth, this is Eddie. What happened to Mom?"

He can tell that she is crying as she tries to tell him. "Oh, Eddie. Mom didn't want you to worry. She's been sick with the cancer for several months. It was in her liver. She suffered. It's a blessing in a way that she doesn't have to suffer any longer."

"Yes, that's true, I suppose. Well, I've got to try to find a bus that heads north. I have a few days of leave, but I don't know right now when I'll be able to get there."

"I'm so glad you'll be able to come. Frank will help me with arranging a service. I'll see you when you get here."

Cancer and she never told him. Would this information have made a difference? Yes. He would have delayed enlisting. But then, the Army was drafting, and he probably still would have ended up here. But maybe, just maybe, he'd have had a few more weeks with his mother, at least enough time to be able to really say goodbye.

He finds a ride into the bus station in the nearby town and buys a series of tickets that, with changes in several cities, will eventually get him to Portland, Maine, in a day and a half. He'll ride all day and all night. Better stock up on some candy bars and an extra pack or two of Camels.

During the daylight, he looks out the window, observing the territory through which he is passing. From small towns, to countryside where crops are growing, to the cities, the landscape changes mile by mile. When darkness comes, he tries to sleep. He is not sure what he feels other than numbness. He can't wrap his head around the reality that his mother won't be greeting him when he arrives in Portland. He'd like to cry, but the tears won't come. He smokes Camel after Camel. He wonders who from Northern Maine will be able to get to Portland for Minnie's funeral?

Finally after what seems an eternity, the bus pulls into the station in Portland. He looks out the window to see if he can spot either Ruth or Frank. Of course, they don't know what bus he'll be on, so it isn't likely they will be at the station. But, look! There they are.

"Ruth. Frank. How did you know to be here?"

"Oh, Eddie." Ruth falls into his arms and cries. "We just took a guess."

"Eddie. How are you doing? You must be pretty tired," says Frank who pats him heartily on the back.

"Frank. I'm doing all right. And you?"

"This is sure hard for Ruth and she's awfully glad you're here. Let me take your bag and we'll head over to the funeral home. The car is just over here."

It is just a short distance from the station to the funeral home. Ruth tells him that she picked out a casket and with Frank's help has made arrangements for Minnie's body to be taken on the train to Caribou where the service will be held. Together, they walk into the parlor where Minnie rests.

Eddie looks down at his mother and finally the tears come. "Mom. Mom, Mom. I never knew. I'm so sorry that I wasn't here." He takes her cold hand in his and looks at the person who has been the most important figure in his life. "I just don't know." He lowers his head and his shoulders shake. Ruth comes over and puts her arm around him. "She was so brave. She never complained. I'm going to miss her so." Brother and sister stand together, locked in grief, unwilling and unable to move.

"Tomorrow's going to be a long day. The train leaves early in the morning. We probably should get home and get something to eat and get you settled in." Frank suggests that they say good night to Minnie.

Once at Ruth's, Eddie finds that he can't sleep. He closes his eyes but images of his mother, dead in her casket, keep coming back and he cries anew. He just can't imagine that she is no longer here. He gets up from the bed, lights a cigarette, and goes to the window. This is the spare room, Minnie's room for the past year. Little of her is here, though. She never had much. Her wicker rocker, he notices, sits in a corner. A picture of her and her sisters as young women sits on the bureau. Her robe and slippers hang neatly on the hook on the door. Minnie was neat; everything had its place.

He looks out the window at the view his mother would have seen for the past year. A street lamp makes some of the neighborhood visible. A lonely car or two parked on the street, a cat prowling across the way. Not much more is visible. Still, it is better to watch than to crawl back into bed and try again to sleep.

Morning comes and his nephews appear at the table. "Boyd. You've grown since I last saw you."

He chuckles because his uncle always says the same thing. "Come on, Uncle Eddie. I just saw you three months ago. I don't think I'm any taller now."

"You sure look it."

"Uncle Eddie, want to see my latest drawings?" Herky, the artist in the family, asks.

"Boy. These are sure good."

"Thanks."

The boys sit at their places and Ruth pours coffee for the adults. She finishes scrambling up the eggs and then puts the platter down on the table.

"How did you sleep?" she asks her brother.

"I didn't. And, you?"

"Oh, you know. Fits and starts. It will just have to do."

As they eat, Ruth and Frank provide details of the arrangements they've taken care of. "We decided to have the service in Caribou since that is where all of Mom's family and friends are. With the gas rationing, we didn't think many folks from the county would be able to make it down here. I know that's a hardship for you, Eddie."

"That's fine. I'll be some tired when I get back to Alabama, but Mom should have a proper funeral. I can sleep on the train and buses."

"I'm so glad you're able to be here, Eddie." Just as she completes the sentiment, a knock on the door announces the arrival of family. "Viola, Fred. You made it. Come in, come in."

"Hi, folks."

"Eddie. You're here!" Viola wraps him in an embrace and he has all he can do to keep himself together. Despite how he used to tease her when she was just a girl, Viola is just like a sister to Eddie, and he is so glad to see her and her husband, Fred, just about the best sort of guy you could ask for.

"We had to wait for the babysitter to come before starting out. We drove most of the night."

"Frank's mother is going to stay with the boys and she should be right along. We've got to hurry to catch the train. Viola, Fred, can I get you a cup of coffee? We have time for that."

The five of them board the train for Caribou, assured by the porter that Minnie's casket is safe in the baggage compartment. It will be many long hours before they'll be home again. They talk quietly, nap, read, look at the passing landscape, and remember Minnie, either silently within or in conversation with each other.

They are small in number but large in hurt as they huddle together outside of the train station in Caribou, waiting for John to arrive to take them to the Colby Baptist Church in Woodland where Minnie's funeral will take place.

John arrives and they pile into his car, tired and numb from the long journey and their recent loss.

"Eddie. Glad you could make it. How's the Army treating you?" John asks.

"I'm getting by."

"Food must not be too good. You're awfully thin," John adds.

"They eat these things called grits. Yuck! I sure miss potatoes."

Once at the church, they join the other mourners and shake many hands. The church choir sings "The Old Rugged Cross" and "Rock of Ages," two of Minnie's favorite hymns. The mourners join in and while singing the words to these familiar songs, Eddie once again remembers times with his mother at this very church, times when he'd restlessly squirm around in his seat and ask Minnie, "When can we leave?" Now, years later, he would give anything to have those days back.

They listen to the words of the pastor, words meant to comfort, but they feel only pain and loss. The service is blessedly short and once ended, mourners file by Minnie's casket for a last goodbye. Eddie walks to Minnie's casket and once again, touches her hand. "Goodbye, Mom. I have to go. If there's a heaven and you're there, please watch out for me. I'm going to a dangerous place soon. I'll be seeing you..." He turns and walks out of the small church to join the others for the graveside service which will be followed by a short reception back at the church. The train schedule dictates the parameters of the day for the five from out of town and soon they'll have to take their leave for the long return journey to Portland.

Once on the train, whose wheels click and clack throughout the night, the travelers try to sleep, gently lulled by the sidewise movement of the train on the tracks. They arrive at the train station in Portland with just enough time for Eddie to get to the adjacent bus station for his trip back to Alabama. A hurried round of goodbyes to family and wishes to stay safe and he is off. As he boards the bus for Alabama, this brief interlude seems like a dream, a dream that hopefully he will wake up from and find that, yes, it was just that—a bad dream. Unfortunately, this is reality and a hard reality, a loss that will have no equal in his lifetime, a lifetime that will in a few short months include several more encounters with death.

Gustaf and Ida Sponberg Dahlgren with family, circa 1902, in Perham, ME. Oldest son, Edward Carl Gustaf Dahlgren is in the back row, 4th from the left.

Edward Carl Gustaf Dahlgren, first Dahlgren born in Northern Maine.
Born October 26, 1876; died October 3, 1915

Almina Anderson Dahlgren. Born July 15, 1888; died June 25, 1943

Edward Carl Dahlgren. Born March 14, 1916; died May 31, 2006.

Chapter Three
The War Years 1943--1945

"As a platoon leader, I did the very best I could to protect my men...with the help of God."
—Edward Carl Dahlgren

"History books will record the accomplishments of the 36ᵗʰ Texas Infantry Division but the two things that will stand out in the memories of its veterans are the mud, through which it invariably had to fight, and the modern Army record for consecutive days of combat which it set at 132 in France."
(http://www.wartimepress.com/archive-article)

Eddie Dahlgren's war in Italy and later on in France reads, as I've said, like the newsreels that precede the movies back home. Except for the two months while recuperating from a shoulder wound in a hospital in Naples, he will be engaged in five major campaigns and experience some of the most terrible fighting in all of Europe: Salerno, Cassino, the Rapido River, Rome, the invasion of Southern France, winter in the Vosges Mountains, Germany and the Siegfried Line, Austria. There will be months where he will experience combat every day, each day waking up wondering, "Is this the day I'm going to be hit?" When his war in Europe ends, he will have spent over a year on the front lines and more than 130 days engaged in direct combat with the Germans. Given that trauma severity is the strongest predictive link to the development of PTSD (Brewin, et al, 2000), is it any surprise that Dahlgren would leave Europe with multiple issues? His war begins in August of 1943 and doesn't end until his death 63 years later...

Shipping Out: August 1943

Eddie returns from his mother's funeral in late June of 1943 and rejoins his unit in Alabama. Given the grinding training schedule, there's no time for grief. Maybe that's for the best. He has no choice but to put the past behind him and move forward. The word around base is that they'll be shipping out to North Africa shortly, thus the intensified training schedule.

Alabama in July is hellishly hot, humid, and buggy. The Texans are used to it, but it is a new experience for this Northern soldier. He doesn't complain but thinks to himself that he probably won't be visiting Alabama in the future...if there is a future for him after the war.

In August, orders come to prepare to ship out and the 36th is off to North Africa. They land at Casablanca and spend the next two weeks in the sands of North Africa, training for the assault on Italy.

September 9, 1943. Packed into small landing boats bobbing in the churning waves, he worries about drowning. That's one way out of this mess, he thinks to himself. But he doesn't drown; he charges ashore with his buddies when his craft hits the beach of Salerno. The weather in Italy is mild, more like a midsummer day in Maine than one in September, the kind of day back home that farmers will be getting ready for the potato harvest and the maple trees will be starting to show off their colors. But now there's no more time to consider the weather.

German troops are waiting for the Americans, waiting with their big guns and tanks. Later he will remember that *"we almost got pushed off the beaches when we landed. The Germans were intent on keeping their territory."* The guns roar and men fall. Earlier in his training, he wondered how he'd react in combat, not knowing if he'd crack or not, but today, he knows he'll be okay. He won't crack. Despite the noise, the cries of fellow soldiers, the blood and flesh flying all around him, he remembers his training and stays calm, moving forward as directed. Despite a fierce fight to keep their territory, the Germans are forced back, and the soldiers of the 36th Infantry Division begin their long march inland.

Boot camp helped prepare me for combat to a certain extent. Without that training, you're in trouble when you go into combat. However, nothing can really prepare you. Things come up in actual combat that you couldn't dream up. It's just way beyond your imagination. It helped me that I'd grown up in the country. I was a good shot. Some of my men were so scared they never fired their rifles. I was a PFC when we landed in Italy and soon was promoted to sergeant. I was good to the men. The men liked me. As sergeant, I had responsibility to look after my men. It keeps things away from your mind, looking after your men.

Eddie Dahlgren's War in Italy

From Salerno, the 36th advances into the lower Liri Valley where they will encounter some of "the most grueling and vicious campaigns in the history of modern warfare" (*Lone Sentry*, 2003, 3). As fall becomes winter, the weather worsens: cold rain becomes wet snow, the mud is wheel-deep and supply trucks bog down. Shoes wear out on the sharp rocks that jut through the snow, and freshly dug foxholes fill with mud almost as soon as they are dug. The 36th is beaten back by the Germans at every turn. The Germans' mines are too concentrated, their machine guns are too plentiful, and their observation points are too exact.

By Christmas Day, December 25, 1943, the Americans are encamped near the Rapido River where they will remain for a month, attempting to take the mountains that the Germans control. Eddie's unit especially wants to take Monte Casino, a monastery that the Germans have fortified and are using as an observation point, enabling them to aim their big guns directly at the advancing Americans.

Fighting continues day and night; the shelling is deafening. Day after day, the men fighting on either side of him fall, hit by enemy bullets. Still, he moves forward as he is told to do, keeping his head down and his rifle at the ready. He continues to think that he'll never come home because of the number of casualties inflicted by the enemy night after night. By New Year's Eve, the weather is growing colder still, and wet snow falls over the terrain. On this night, the end of the old year and the beginning of a new one, he says to himself, "*If I ever get home, every New Year's Eve I'll stay home by a warm stove, with a good book and a good light...no guns, no noise, no more death.*"

The battle for Monte Cassino continues into the winter but is over for him on the night of February 11, 1944, when a German bullet hits him in the shoulder. After feigning death through the night while the German snipers slash through the area, looking for enemy wounded, he manages to make his way off the mountain, following a mule supply trail once daylight comes. He'll spend the next two months in a hospital in Naples.

"Somewhere in Italy"

April 18, 1944

Dear Viola,

Thought it about time to drop you a line. Heard from Ruth you aren't feeling so well. What seems to be the trouble? [He didn't know that Viola was experiencing morning sickness due to her pregnancy.] *I am okay now. They patch a guy up pretty good. If I can get by now until this thing is over, I'll be satisfied. How are Fred and the kids these days? John is up home again now. Ruth said he was going to keep house. I should think he would board out wouldn't you. Heard from Grace, Douglas, Bill Buzzell so have been getting quite a lot of mail.*

Tell Junior to write me a letter. He must have some time. How are Fred's hens laying? Cost me 24 cents for just one egg over here. Some price, huh! Had two fried eggs and potatoes Sunday. Soon will be time for you folks to start putting in your garden, I suppose. It is real nice over here now for a change. We got a

Hersey bar tonight. Quite a treat. Are you going to have any vacation this summer? You sure need a rest, don't you? Suppose it's hard to leave the children though.

Allen C. is in India. Tom Skidgel is in England. I wonder when they are going to start this invasion they're talking about. Ralph Anderson is still in the states. Going to get a furlough he says.
Hope this finds you better.

> *Love to you all,*
> *Eddie*

He runs out of space on the small patch of paper allowed for this sort of communication but in looking it over is satisfied that he's said just enough to Viola to reassure her that he is doing as well as he can. He could have told her about the Purple Heart he'd received from his hospital bed for the shoulder injury he'd suffered at Cassino. Oh, well. Looking over his reference to Fred's hens, he lets himself long for home and a fresh egg, a hot cup of coffee, and the comfort of family. Who knows when—or if—this will be in his future. What he knows for certain, though, is that in a few short days, he will rejoin his unit and be back in the thick of it.

The last two years, I carried a Thompson sub-machine gun. I asked if I could use one and was given permission. The Tommy gun was lighter than my rifle and more effective at close range and when you pressed the trigger, 30 bullets came out. It was quite the weapon.
The worst was night patrol. The captain would call over to me and say, 'Eddie, pick four men and go out.' I was a platoon leader at this point. With all of the constant German shelling, we lost a lot of men. You'd get really tired, played out, and pull back for a while. But you knew you'd have to go back. You get so tired, so discouraged that after a while, you take chances that you probably shouldn't. I got away with it. Others got hit.

Heading for France

Eddie Dahlgren rejoins his unit in May and is immediately immersed in heavy fighting in Anzio. From Anzio, his unit moves inland and in one of the battles in the Alban Hills outside of Rome, he will be awarded his first Bronze Star and a promotion. On May 25, his unit is encamped in densely wooded hills just outside of the town of Velletri, a key stronghold in the German line defending Rome. In the night, the Americans creep around and over the top of Mount Artemisio, trapping a German garrison (*Lone Sentry*, 5). There is now nothing stopping the Americans from entering Rome.

"We went through Rome on trucks at midnight. People were crowding the streets, waving at us. The Germans had pulled out. They didn't destroy the city."

In June of 1944, as Eisenhower's troops are landing in Normandy, the Seventh Army, including the 36th Infantry, is moving swiftly up the Italian peninsula, heading for the south of France. In the eleven months of the Italian campaign, the 36th counts 11,000 casualties and many thousands more wounded by enemy guns. They encounter the Germans along the way and engage them in "short, sharp, decisive battles" (*Lone Sentry,* 5). On August 15, 1944, those able-bodied soldiers of the 36th who are still in the fight land in Southern France at the port city of Toulon just east of Marseille.

Shortly after landing, his unit will head north and east in an attempt to drive the Germans out of France. In eight days, they travel 250 miles, reaching Montelimar where they encounter a Panzer division and are hammered for eight days. The 36th, victorious, pushes forward toward the Moselle River, swollen by heavy winter rains. Only one intact bridge, a hastily constructed temporary one at that, spans the Moselle in the area where the 36th is fighting the Germans. With casualties high, 1700 in September alone, and with battle experiences constant, Eddie Dahlgren's leadership skills earn him a series of promotions which will eventually advance him to the position of platoon leader and the rank of sergeant in just a few short weeks.

In September on the edge of the Vosges Mountains in the south of France near a small village named Tendon, the 36th will wage a battle against the Germans that will last more than two weeks with no break in the fighting which even goes on through the nighttime hours. The Germans have heavily mined the hillsides where vineyards used to flourish. Night patrols are ambushed regularly by German reconnaissance fighters. Nazi artillery pours down heavily on the Americans trying to find cover in the hillside forests.

This will be the most intense fighting that Dahlgren will experience during his entire war and he will earn a Silver Star for his courageous action in rescuing a wounded buddy from an enemy mine field. These memories of his close encounter with death will return again and again, haunting him worse than any of the other episodes of his war. Because he is never able to talk about this episode, other than to say he rescued a buddy caught in a minefield, the following narrative is an imagined approximation as to how his day in Tendon might have been...

Few people outside of the area would be able to tell an outsider where the village of Tendon is located, it's that small. Those who live there, peacefully up until the Germans invaded, make their way in life by tending to their vineyards and flocks of sheep. Bucolic and bountiful before the war, Tendon's fields of corn will turn into killing fields. The Germans plant mines in the many fields surrounding the village, hoping to pick off and discourage the American troops that are coming north. Among those heading north are the soldiers of the 36th. Now in the position of platoon leader, it is Dahlgren's duty to try to keep his men safe as they cross the countryside.

"I'm going first," he might say. "Follow me and you'll be okay. Fall in behind me. Don't step off my path. We know that the Germans have likely planted mines in the fields." He starts off, slowly and carefully, observing every minute feature of the ground in front of him. If he suspects a mine,

he nudges the area with a stick and can only hope that there won't be an explosion.

It seems like it takes hours to cross the few acres of open terrain that reminds him of the potato fields of home in Maine. Once on the other side, he keeps looking back at his men as they make their way toward him. Suddenly, there is the sickening sound of a loud explosion and a body, missing an arm, is thrown up into the air only to fall a short distance from the explosion. "Help me. Help me!" The soldier behind the one who is surely dead is crying out, "I'm hit. I can't move. I'm scared!"

"Just wait where you are. I'll get you." Dahlgren can't help but recognize that the other man has stepped on a mine that he himself had just missed as he paced his way across the field. He wonders how many other mines might be just a footprint away. He can't afford to think any longer. It is up to him to rescue this man and the others behind him. If he steps on a mine this time through, it's just meant to be.

The grass is high, and it is difficult to see clearly where he and the others had crossed on their first time through the field. He knows he is tempting death by going back through this field again but he has a job to do and it must be done. As he enters the field, several other soldiers following the one who is waiting to be rescued, start gingerly moving forward, hoping to step exactly in the same places that the others before them had stepped. Again, an explosion. Again, a body missing limbs flies into the air and lands close by, close enough to Dahlgren to deposit bits of flesh and blood on his uniform and his face. He continues. Just a few more yards, and he'll be able to get his comrade.

"Hang on. I'm almost there." How is he ever going to be able to support this man and avoid stepping on a mine? Four boots crossing together means more of a likelihood of stepping on something than the two boots of a solitary soldier.

He reaches the wounded soldier. "Here. Put your arm over my shoulder. Let me have your rifle. Can you walk?"

"I think I can."

"Let's go." Dahlgren calls out to the rest of his squad. "Everyone behind us. Follow my footsteps. We'll get across. It's not too far."

He desperately hopes that they'll all make it safely to the side of the field and that he'll not lose any more men today. One step at a time, cautious as a hunted animal, Dahlgren and his wounded comrade eventually reach safety on the other side of the field. He carefully helps his buddy to the ground where a medic can then check him out. He turns back to the field and watches intently until every man is safely across. Now he can breathe and maybe have a cigarette.

The fall and early winter of 1944 in the Vosges Mountains in France is the worst fighting he's seen to date, intense and never ending, with the Germans securely entrenched behind the Moselle River and in the forests of the Vosges, which they have heavily mined. Their heavy guns roar day and night, sometimes hitting the wooden homes with thatched roofs, igniting fires. Flames, ash and smoke provide a contrast to the dark hills and skeletal trees of winter. "Every yard of the Vosges had to be wrenched from the obstinate enemy" (*Lone Sentry*, 8). Firefights would last for hours when Americans on patrol would meet German observers who would then radio back to "Nazi artillery units which poured down deadly tree bursts on the unprotected Yanks" (*Lone Sentry,* 8). His unit will go unrelieved for four months with no break in the action. American losses continue to mount: 1700 casualties in September, 2000 in October. The only way out of this war is to be killed or be wounded. At one point in the action, his platoon which at full strength numbers fifty men, has only ten of the original men left and he has to go back for replacements.

He and his remaining men walk back ten miles in the rain into a valley and march into the town where they'll find these replacements. A first lieutenant says to him, "Sergeant Dahlgren, go up and down the line and pick your men. Pick forty and keep the men you have with you now." As he looks over the prospects, he notes how young many of them look. Could he have ever been that young, that unseasoned? Some can't be more than seventeen and look as if they have yet to need to shave. Unlike his own and his ten veterans' uniforms which are encrusted with dirt and dried blood, these young men's uniforms are clean. He knows as he picks his men that he could very well be deciding their fate. It is a heavy responsibility but he has a duty to pick from the line. As he looks at his prospects, he sees fear in some eyes, excitement in others. He knows the look of fear and knows the debilitating effect of fear on a soldier. And he knows that these young soldiers with excitement in their eyes are especially vulnerable because they'll take risks that kill or maim. "You, you, you, you He points his index finger at individuals and randomly selects. They sleep in a barn for the night. The next morning, they are sent back to the front.

He worries about how these new, untried members of his platoon will do and how he will ever be able to keep them safe. He tells himself that he will do the best he can, and with the help of God, they will all get home again.

One of the young replacements was just so scared. There was shelling during the day and through the night. We dug into a fox hole. There were three of us: the young one, another old timer like me, and me. We put the young fellow in the middle. He was hit in the night and killed. We stayed still throughout the night.

Lily Marlene
(English lyrics by Tommie Connor, 1944)

Underneath the lantern,
By the barrack gate
Darling I remember
The way you used to wait
T'was there that you whispered tenderly,
That you loved me,
You'd always be,
My Lilli of the Lamplight,
My own Lilli Marlene

Time would come for roll call,
Time for us to part,

Darling I'd caress you
And press you to my heart,
And there 'neath that far-off lantern light,
I'd hold you tight,
We'd kiss good night,
My Lilli of the Lamplight,
My own Lilli Marlene

Orders came for sailing,
Somewhere over there
All confined to barracks
Was more than I could bear
I knew you were waiting in the street
I heard your feet,
But could not meet,
My Lilli of the Lamplight,
My own Lilly Marlene

Resting in our billets,
Just behind the lines
Even tho' we're parted,
Your lips are close to mine
You wait where that lantern softly gleams,
Your sweet face seems
To haunt my dreams
My Lilli of the Lamplight,
My own Lilli Marlene.

When the army passes through small French towns, the sounds of popular songs coming from local inns can be heard on the street, making the passing soldiers long for a warm place by the inn's fire and perhaps a glass of something that might take the sting of war away for a short while. Often it is "Lily Marlene" that is playing on the jukebox, sung by a husky-voiced girl singer. The song with its haunting lines of a soldier recalling his time with a special girl "underneath the lantern by the garden gate" is sung in French, English, and German and claimed by all three armies as their own symbol of the universal longing of soldiers for the arms of a loved one embracing them in the cold of night.

Sometimes at night in the freshly dug foxholes that are as cold as the coldest potato cellars in Northern Maine, Eddie Dahlgren allows himself a moment to think of home. Now a hardened veteran who has seen too much violence and unrelenting bloodshed, he doesn't really expect to see home again. It is just a matter of time before it is his turn to take a lethal bullet. A man can tempt fate only so often before he draws a losing hand.

He's cold and tired. The temperature hovers at freezing or just below, warm enough to make for wet foxholes and constantly damp clothing. He is as afraid of drowning with the rising water in the foxholes as he is of being hit by an enemy round. In Northern Maine where he grew up, he never learned to swim. The brooks and streams he fished in were never deep enough to require him to swim, as long as he was careful and watchful of currents and the swelling that the spring brought to the waters.

He never really sleeps for more than a few minutes when some movement jars him awake and he's back on alert, trying to detect the source of the noise. Often it is the skulking movement of rats and their incessant chewing that jars him awake. Rats thrive on war and make no judgments about friend or foe; flesh is flesh and the smell of blood draws them out when the soldiers quiet down at night. He hates their musky smell, their beady yellow eyes and sleek fur made damp by the moisture in the foxholes. He abhors hearing them moving in the night, seeking out an unprotected finger or ankle. Rats don't care if the flesh is dead or alive. They need to eat to live.

As his army plods north, the mail from home is sporadic but when mail call comes and there is a letter from home, a soldier's day becomes like Christmas. In early January, he receives a letter from his sister. Although it is good to read her news, some of the news is not so good and will mean that when and if he ever gets home, one less loved one will be there to welcome him back. His sister's letter announces that Grammie died on Christmas Eve at age ninety. She had outlived her husband, two sons and two daughters-in-law. Healthy up until the very end, she was able to live in her own house and tend to her own kitchen until she simply weakened and took to her bed, never to rise again. This was Grammie of the warm, soft molasses cookies and ample lap that had comforted him and loved him unconditionally. He will miss her.

By late January, 1945, his unit reaches the Moder River in Alsace-Lorraine in the East of France, an area that over the centuries goes back and forth from German to French domain, depending on the victorious army of the time. In recent history, a part of France until the Germans invaded at the beginning of the war, it is currently occupied by German troops. Near Bischwiller, France, a small town north of the Vosges Mountains, he once again displays uncommon courage and receives a second Bronze Star for leading a squad of nineteen men in knocking out two German machine gun nests.

In early February, the 2nd platoon of Company E of the 36th Division attacks the German forces occupying the small river village of Oberhoffen. In fierce house-to-house fighting, the Americans suffer heavy losses. Over the next several days, the Germans will be successful in surrounding and outnumbering the Americans who radio for rescue.

Located just outside the perimeter of the village, Sergeant Dahlgren's 3rd platoon is ordered to advance into Oberhoffen to rescue the surrounded unit. At 6 a.m. on the morning of February 11, with a cold drizzle falling on them and visibility poor, he swiftly organizes his men and moves forward to contact the 2nd platoon. Something about the atmospheric conditions produced by the drizzle produces the familiar smell of potatoes, a mainstay in the diet of the desperate civilians who are reduced to being cellar dwellers in their own homes. The smell is a bittersweet reminder of the life he'd left just a few months ago. Enough of the reminiscing. He senses that this will be a day when he needs to have all of his attention focused on the moment... if he is to have any chance of making it out alive from the mud and cold of the moment. His instincts are to prove accurate. At any juncture during the heavy fighting for control of Oberhoffen on this day, he could easily become another casualty of this long and bloody war. Best to keep his wits about him, think of the men who are depending on him to keep them safe, and get the day over with.

One of his men that day is another Maine native, a young man from Presque Isle, married with two young sons whose pictures are safe in the inside pocket of their father's army jacket. Thomas Kersey is one of the replacements that Sergeant Dahlgren selected from the line outside of Tendon several weeks ago. Sometimes in the evening when all is quiet, the two Mainers speculate about what is going on back home. "I sure miss my boys. I'm sure they've grown a lot since I last saw them. Don't know if they'll even know me when I get back...if I get back." Their dad is a good soldier, one Dahlgren can always count on to be there when needed.

His company crosses the swollen banks of the Moder and with boots drenched by the freezing water of the river, they continue on into the village. There isn't much for cover. The trees in winter are bare of leaves and there is much open land between the houses. They can see and smell smoke rising from burning roof tops where German guns have hit their targets. All that is left of the town are the shattered walls of houses.

They are crossing a field and in the distance, German soldiers can be seen. A shot rings out, close this time to Dahlgren's helmet. He hears a thud and looks. "Oh, God, no, no, no." Kersey is down with a bullet clean through his helmet. Dead. Now the cool and calculating Dahlgren is enraged. This war has turned personal and today, he will end it one way or another.

He continues to lead his men into the town, commanding them to stay low, to stay alert for any movement. He splits his group in half when they reach a small street whose sign announces that this is "Rue l'Hiver," Winter Street. "You men, take the left. Watch out. We don't know where the Germans are hiding." He leads his small squad up the right hand side of the street. He looks up towards the end of the street where he sees a group of Germans crossing a field. "Take cover, men," he yells and dashes into a barn. He moves into position by a small window and opens fire with his sub-machine gun. Six enemy soldiers fall dead, several others groan with the pain of bullet wounds. Those who remain standing appear dazed and disorganized, unable to ascertain where the firing is coming from. Laying down a torrent of accurate fire, he kills six more of the enemy, wounds several others and completely disorganizes the hostile force. He orders a rifleman with an automatic weapon to remain and cover the field while he leads his platoon forward, through intermittent enemy sniper fire, to make contact with the 2nd platoon. Part of their mission is accomplished but both platoons still have to get to safety and to do that, they must now prepare for what is sure to be a German counterattack.

Eddie Dahlgren is again on the move, leading his men along Winter Street. As he approaches a house on the end of the street, the Germans suddenly open fire with machine pistols and rifles. Moving in the face of hostile fire, he runs toward the building, hurls a grenade through the door and, bursting into the house, fires his sub-machine gun into the midst of the startled Germans he finds there. The entire group of eight enemy soldiers quickly surrenders. As he starts toward the next house, he is fired on by a hostile machine gun set up in one of the windows. Jumping back into the house which he has just cleared, he secures rifle grenades from one of his men and, although the two buildings are only a few feet apart and the angle of fire great, he begins discharging grenades at the difficult target. Although he is exposed to fire from the enemy gun, he remains in position at a window and continues launching grenades until he destroys the machine gun and kills its two crew members.

Sergeant Dahlgren then moves to the rear of the house and, while exposed to the enemy in the doorway, a second machine gun emplacement in a nearby barn starts firing directly at him. He swiftly hurls a hand grenade into the barn and then rushes the position, again firing his sub-machine gun as he runs. He overwhelms resistance in the barn and captures five Germans, three of whom have been wounded by his accurate fire. Skillfully reorganizing his men to continue the attack, he again moves toward the house where the machine gun which he destroyed was emplaced. When his group is again fired on by hostile riflemen, he enters the enemy-held house by a window and, opening fire with his weapon, traps the Germans in a cellar. Hurling several grenades into the midst of the enemy, he wounds several Germans and captures ten prisoners. Moving forward aggressively, he leads his men in clearing all the houses up to a road junction.

At this point, Eddie Dahlgren and a companion decide to start down the street to the right and check the houses for more of the enemy troops. Although they advance down the street without attracting enemy fire, Sergeant Dahlgren hears German voices in one of the houses. After his companion fires two rifle grenades at the building, Dahlgren dashes into the house where the Germans have fled to the cellar. Kicking open the cellar door, he fires several bursts and calls for the enemy to surrender. Sixteen hostile soldiers file out with their hands up. Sergeant Dahlgren then rejoins his men and leads them in clearing the remainder of the houses on the street. By this time he personally has killed at least eight Germans, wounded many more and captured 39 prisoners of war. His bold leadership and his outstanding personal courage on this long day in Oberhoffen are responsible for eliminating a serious threat to the 2nd platoon and for repelling an enemy attack.

Many long hours later, this nightmare of a day finally draws to an end. Night finds him cold, tired, hungry, and too desensitized at this point in his war to realize the danger he's been in all day. Dahlgren just wants to lean against a solid wall, smoke a cigarette and relish a quiet interlude of no guns firing and no men dying. He reaches into his shirt pocket for his pack of cigarettes, his hands shaking badly, extracts a cigarette, then realizes that he doesn't have a match.

"Here, Eddie. Let me get that for you." One of his men reaches across the space between them and, striking a match, holds it up for Eddie.

"Thank you. Quite a day, huh?" They sit and smoke, breathing in and breathing out. At this moment, thankfully, there is nothing else to do.

Dahlgren's disregard for his own safety and skillful leadership on this day are noticed by his men and the men from the 2nd platoon that he has rescued. Sensing that his actions are above and beyond the call of duty, several of these men, including 2nd Lieutenant Eugene M. Perry, Jr., platoon leader of the surrounded 2nd platoon, will write affidavits in support of Dahlgren being nominated to receive the Medal of Honor.

Another Promotion

The war continues and the 36th continues to be heavily engaged in the combat. From Oberhoffen, they will chase the retreating Germans across the Rhine and into Austria. Dahlgren learns in mid-March that he is being considered for the Medal of Honor and that he is being promoted again, this time into the officer ranks as a second lieutenant.

"Dahlgren! The captain wants to see you."

He walks quickly over to the command tent. A snappy salute and then, "Sir. You want to see me?"

"Yes, Sergeant Dahlgren. Congratulations on your promotion to second lieutenant. We think you'll agree that the best part of this promotion is a chance for a little 'R&R' away from the front at officers' training school just south of Paris. You'll be gone for five weeks or so. Get packed and report back ASAP. The train leaves in just a couple of hours. And, I think you've already heard that you're being recommended for the Medal of Honor? By all accounts, you certainly earned this award. All of the paperwork should be done on that by the time you return. Congratulations for a job well done."

"Thank you, sir. That's great. I'll be ready when the train gets here."

It is March 14, 1945—his twenty-ninth birthday.

During the weeks away from his unit, Eddie Dahlgren learns quickly what he needs to know in order to carry out his duties as a second lieutenant. Despite the relative safety of being away from the front, he finds that he isn't able to relax. Sleep doesn't come easily, his hands shake, and he stutters when he speaks. He worries about his men and is anxious to get back to check in on them. By mid-April, decked out in new uniforms and wearing the silver lieutenant bars on his hat and shoulders, he boards yet another train, this one heading east to his old unit.

Once settled in "back home," he takes time to write to his Uncle John.

> *April 22, 1945*
> *"Germany"*

Dear John,

Well I find I have a little time so thought I would drop you a few lines to let you know I am still around and feeling fine. How are you these days? O.K. I hope. I've had it pretty easy for the past five or six weeks. Been going to school down around Paris. They made me an officer so had to go to school. Guess they must be getting hard up for officers. Back with my old outfit again now. I imagine Viola is there with you now. Well, you shouldn't be lonesome. Lots of children around. This country is very nice. The weather is wonderful. Don't know why these damn Germans wanted so much more land. Doesn't seem to be very thickly populated around here anyway. Well, the Russians are in Berlin. We should hook up with them now. Don't see how the war can last very much longer. How is Freddie making out selling insurance? Heard he didn't pass his physical for the Army. Bet he was glad. How is Albert these days? Should be home on a furlough before too damn long even if the war doesn't end soon. Will close for now.

> *Best Regards,*
> *Eddie*

In late April word comes to him that he's been approved to receive the Medal of Honor. Despite this information, his war goes on as before: he is constantly cold and wet, living on canned rations, waking up each day still amazed to find himself breathing and wondering why he's survived when others haven't. Even though the Germans are now in retreat, he can't allow himself to believe that he might make it home alive.

When the war ends in early May, he and his unit are part of the occupying army, stationed in Ulm, Germany where the giant cathedral is the only relic to have survived Allied bombing.

In July, he learns he's to be sent home so he can attend a White House ceremony with several other soldiers who will at the same time receive their Medals of Honor from the President of the United States. It looks like his war is over...at least for now.

Private Edward Dahlgren, May, 1944, in hospital in Naples, recuperated from gunshot wound to shoulder.

Oberhoffen/Moder

Oberhoffen, France, February 12, 1945. Mud and destruction rule the day.

Oberhoffen/Moder

Rue de la gare

Rue principale

Oberhoffen, France, February 12, 1945. American soldiers walk down the main street, Rue Principale and Rue de la gare where the train station used to be.

Oberhoffen/Moder
Rue de la Forêt

Route de
Schirrheim

Oberhoffen, France, February 12, 1945. More scenes of destruction and captured German soldiers.

Oberhoffen/Moder Maison Guillaume GROSS

Maison Guillaume
GROSS

Route de Bischwiller

Oberhoffen, France, February 12, 1945. A soldier survives the day and another dies. Others are wounded and carried back to Bischwiller for medical care.

La gan

Jeux d'enfants parmi les décombr rue Principale. Robert Birgel et Marcelle Sonntag-Sachot.

Oberhoffen, France, late February, 1945. Alsatian children regard the spoils of war.

Sgt. Edward Dahlgren, February, 1945. The cost of many battles are evident.

Chapter Four
The Long Way Home 1945–1949

A Ceremony with the President

In mid-July, Eddie Dahlgren takes a train out of Ulm and arrives in Paris to await a plane which will take him and several other Medal of Honor nominees home to the United States. Once across the wide Atlantic, the plane flies over eastern Canada and Northern Maine. "Hey, Eddie! There's Maine down below. Want to jump out?" He laughs at the comment from his new buddy, Charles MacGillivary of Massachusetts, a fellow Medal of Honor nominee who lost both legs in Europe. It's July 10. In a very short time, this plane will touch down in New York, and he will be back on American soil. Once off the plane, he heads with his duffel bag to the bus station where he will take a bus to Portland, Maine, to his sister Ruth Riley's home where he will stay until August 11.

Just before boarding the bus to Maine, a reporter who has learned that Medal of Honor nominees have come in on the plane just in from Paris, asks Dahlgren to talk about the Medal. Still in shock at simply being back on American soil, he briefly sums up the story of the battle at Oberhoffen, France, where his action took out three enemy machine gun emplacements and rescued an American platoon. "I feel a man needs plenty of luck to get the Congressional Medal of Honor and stay alive to receive it," is his answer to the reporter's question. That question answered for now, what will plague him for the rest of his life is the harder question of why he was spared when so many of his fellow soldiers died in battle.

During the month back in Maine, prior to leaving for Washington, D.C., he fills his days with walks on the beach at Pine Point and with matinees at the local movie house. He smokes incessantly, stutters when speaking, and shakes uncontrollably at night while trying to sleep, troubled by nightmares about the war. In his dreams, he sees German soldiers crossing a field. He hears the crack of enemy guns and listens for the explosion that will soon come. He can't eat, and his hands shake so much he splashes coffee out of his cup when he tries to drink. Already forty pounds lighter than when he went off to war, he continues to lose weight and has developed jaundice, his pale skin now tinged a sickly yellow.

On his second day at his sister's home, he doubles over with an intense pain in his lower back. A local doctor diagnoses kidney stones and tells him that about all he can do is take a pain reliever and hope that the stone passes out of his system sooner rather than later. He goes to the VA, thinking that the kidney stone attack must be related to his war since he's never had a problem with them before. He is told he must prove a connection; discouraged that he can't, he gives up. This attack will be the first in a lifelong battle with kidney stones.

A reporter from the local paper telephones Ruth and asks if her brother might be willing to sit for an interview. Although reluctant to talk, his sister convinces him that he should let people know about his experiences "over there." While awaiting President Truman's return to D.C. from the Big Three Conference in Potsdam, he eventually agrees to speak with the reporter Katherine A. Connolly from the Portland newspaper. When she asks him about being a hero, he replies, "When instinct and a little temper make a fellow want to even things up with the Germans, that's not heroism—that's human nature" (Connolly, 1945). Despite his modest response to Connelly's question, official records of numerous awards for gallantry and heroic achievement in action mark him as one of the nation's "most outstanding war heroes" (Connolly, 1945).

During his 26 months overseas, his leadership ability is demonstrated repeatedly, leading to rapid promotions from private first class when he landed with his platoon in Italy to second lieutenant after his action at Oberhoffen. When asked to describe what happened at Oberhoffen, he tells Connolly about being a platoon leader of a group of only eighteen men charged with trying to rescue an overrun platoon surrounded by German SS troops holed up in about twenty-five houses along one particular street in the town. "From the racket our men were making throughout the town, I guess the Germans figured their opposition was plenty strong. If they had known of the odds against my particular position, we would have been dead ducks. But they didn't until it was too late and that's why I'm living to tell about it." He goes on to pass on praise to "all the soldiers coming in from other angles who scared hell out of the Germans. It made it easier for my men to move ahead." (Connolly, 1945)

He leaves Portland on August 11 for Washington, D.C., where a large group of Medal of Honor recipients are gathering for a ceremony to be held in the East Room of the White House upon President Truman's return to the States. Because the ceremony is delayed until August 23, he has time to get to know the other recipients and attend the Washington Senators' home games. He stays at the Army War College barracks and eats mess hall food. Not sure about civilian employment, he is counting his pennies and won't splurge on a restaurant meal.

Once informed about the date for the ceremony, he calls his sister Ruth who will drive to Washington with her husband, Frank, to attend the event. On the morning of August 23, twenty-eight soldiers who are to receive a grateful nation's highest military honor from President Truman gather in the East Room. Arranged in rows with a center aisle for the President's entrance into the room, the men stare solemnly at the camera for the official group portrait. Those in wheelchairs occupy the first row. Lieutenant Dahlgren sits two rows back in an aisle seat and when the President enters, he stops for a picture, placing his hand on the back of Dahlgren's seat. Dahlgren's uniform jacket sports a row of ribbons and the second lieutenant bars he earned in action. Thin but erect, he looks straight ahead.

As each of the soldiers is called forward, his official citation is read. Then the President places the Medal around the neck of each recipient. He speaks directly to Lieutenant Dahlgren, "I'd rather wear this award than be President of the United States. Congratulations, Lieutenant." Dahlgren bows his head slightly, demonstrating his respect for the President, and then returns to his seat. He thinks about his mother, wishing that she could have been with him and wondering what she would have thought of her son. "Mom, I'm a long way from home still. And I still can't believe I'm sitting in this room safe from harm, meeting the President of the United States. I suppose it will take some time to sink in."

After the ceremony and reception, he is approached by a reporter. "What are your plans now, Lieutenant?"

"I'm hoping to be discharged from the Army as soon as possible. I've done my job. This business is finished." He expresses an interest in taking advantage of the G.I. Bill. "I was a machinist before the war. I think I'd like to be a civil engineer."

He turns to his sister. "Ruth? I think I'm ready to head home. Is that okay with you?"

"Yes, Eddie. We can go home now."

"Lowell Thomas Broadcasts Story
of Lt. Ed Dahlgren over NBC Network"
(article in *Bangor Daily News,* Sept. 1945)

"He killed eight Germans, captured thirty-nine, wounded many more, stormed more than four buildings alone. No wonder they are decorating him," Lowell Thomas, well known radio commentator, concluded recently as he broadcasted the story of how 2nd Lt. Edward C. Dahlgren of Caribou earned the coveted Congressional Medal of Honor, which he was awarded by President Truman at Washington a few weeks ago."

What follows are more of Lowell Thomas's words, describing Dahlgren's heroic action, words which were heard over the facilities of the National Broadcasting Company:

"Among the arrivals in Washington today was a second lieutenant of the Infantry. Next week this Second Louey will receive the Congressional Medal of Honor and here is the tale of how he earned it.

On the eleventh day of last February, Second Lt. Ed Dahlgren of Caribou, Maine, the leader of a platoon of the 142nd regiment, the 36th Infantry Division, near Oberhoffen in France, was in the vanguard of a counterattack. The Nazis had placed snipers in the doorways of one particular house. Without considering their number, Lt. Dahlgren rushed the door alone, jumped inside firing his tommy gun to clear the place. Then he went back to the front door, snatched a grenade-launcher from one of his men and with a hand grenade, he silenced the machine gun that had been firing from a house down the street. Having done that, he went back to the back door of the house and rushed a barn twenty yards distant where another machine gun was firing. When he was near the door of the barn he threw a grenade and wounded or captured the entire crew manning the machine gun. In the first house, Dahlgren captured eight Germans. In the barn he killed six more, wounding others, and five more surrendered. Then this rampaging Second Louey from Caribou, Maine, went into still a third house and with his rifle grenade, he drove the Germans into the cellar, whereupon alone he kicked open the cellar door. Firing his submachine gun, he warned them to surrender and come out. The upshot of it was that sixteen Germans came up with their hands back of their necks. For that, Second Lt. Edward C. Dahlgren of Caribou, Maine, who was a machinist working in Worcester, Massachusetts, before the war, joins that fine small band of men who wear the Congressional Medal of Honor. Before going to France, he was wounded in action in Italy.
He killed eight Germans, captured thirty nine, wounded many more, stormed more than four buildings alone. No wonder they are decorating him."

The Train North
November, 1945

When he returns from Washington, Eddie Dahlgren continues to walk along the Atlantic shore close to his sister's home in South Portland, looking eastward to where he'd been. Born inland, he finds that he misses the streams and rolling hills of Northern Maine. Portland holds opportunities for work, for education, for entertainment, but he doesn't feel "at home" there. He tells his sister he is going back to Aroostook County. Before he leaves, he keeps two appointments: one with his sister's dentist and another to a local photographer.

The government-issued dentures that have been with him throughout the war are now so very loose that they cause mouth cankers. He thinks that the dentist might be able to make some adjustment for a better fit. This very kind and patriotic dentist goes one better, supplying him with the best dentures that he knows how to make, for no charge. "After all you've done for us, this is the least I can do for you, Lieutenant Dahlgren." Humbled by this unexpected gift, Dahlgren stutters a thank you.

The second appointment of the day, made at his sister's urging, is a sitting for a portrait in his dress uniform. Although still very thin, Eddie Dahlgren is a handsome subject with dark wavy hair and the trademark Dahlgren smile, the one that tips up a bit higher on the right. A few days later, he is packed and ready for the long trip to Northern Maine. It is November 5, 1945.

The train ride north takes many hours, what with all of the stops along the way. He stares out the window, looking at the passing landscape. The once colorful trees are now drab without their leaves. He supposes that the potato harvest will soon be winding down. He isn't sure what to expect when the ride is done, and he gets off the train in Caribou. He knows he can stay with his Uncle John until he finds work and can afford to live on his own. He looks forward to visiting Viola and Fred and their growing family. A new baby, a girl they named Cynthia, had arrived while he was in Europe.

Finally the train pulls into the station in Caribou. At nine o'clock in the evening, he gets out of his seat and pulls his duffel from the rack above his head. All that he owns is in this one bag. He straightens his uniform jacket, checks his tie and tucks it more securely inside his shirt, and pulls his hat just a bit to the right. He walks down the aisle, behind the women and their children who chatter excitedly as they recognize grandparents waving to them from the platform.

He descends the two steps from the train, taking his time and placing each foot carefully and securely on the step. His legs still sometimes threaten to give up their support of his thin body. He takes a deep breath of the cool fall air and looks up. Caribou, Maine, says the sign on the station's building. He recognizes the sign and the station from his high school days when he'd descended similar steps and headed towards the high school building with his sister and cousin Viola.

"Eddie. Over here." He turns his head toward the voice. Uncle John. The voice is still the same, but John is grayer and thinner. "Viola is waiting at home. She can't leave the children, but she is sure looking forward to seeing you." Eddie puts his duffel down and extends his hand to John. "Welcome home, Eddie."

No band. No speeches. No keys to the city. And that's just fine. Eddie isn't one for fanfare. He just wants to go home, such as it is.

Duty Calls

In the duffel bag he carries north, he's stashed the money he's saved from his military pay from the past two years. Already his savings have been diminished by the expenses he incurred in Washington, waiting for the Medal of Honor ceremony. He hopes that he has enough left to be able to buy a reliable used car. And he wants to be able to offer Viola money to cover his room and board. Not expecting that he'll have enough money to buy civilian clothes, he is content to wear the khaki uniform pants that he's worn for the past few years. He knows that none of his civilian clothes will fit him now that he is so thin, and he's heard about how hard it is to buy even one white shirt. Shortages are everywhere for everything: not enough jobs to go around, not enough homes, not enough cars. He knows he needs to find a job quickly and is counting on working in the potato houses during the winter for a source of income. Not only does he need the money that a job will provide, he needs the routine and structure that a job brings. He has too much free time on his hands and all too often, thoughts of the war he left behind intrude on his peace of mind.

But for today, duty calls and he has two important appointments to keep. He asks to borrow his Uncle John's car for the day and drives the several miles to where he had grown up and to where his mother is now buried. He recalls the last time he saw her alive, standing on the stairs of his sister's house, trying to hold back tears as she said goodbye to her son who was going off to boot camp. He misses her now and wishes fervently that he'd had more time to visit with her that day. If he'd known she was ill, would he have said anything more or done anything else? Would he have hugged her a minute longer or said anything more tender than "Love you"? They were not a demonstrative family; maybe a few more minutes would probably have been spent making small talk, avoiding any mention of the war that he would be joining in a few short weeks.

He slows down as he approaches the cemetery, located in the small town of Woodland. Viola had told him to turn right at the third lane and go almost to the end. The marker will be on the left, next to Edward's stone. He turns into the lane and slowly drives towards the back of the cemetery. Anderson is the name on the big stone, marking Minnie's parents' grave. Just behind this stone will be his father's stone...and now Minnie's.

He'd given Ruth money to purchase a stone he had yet to see. He wonders what she's chosen, knowing that the small amount of money they'd had available wouldn't buy anything elaborate.

Ruth has done well. The stone complements his father's stone quite well, making it seem like they belong together, just as the couple had belonged together in life. He kneels down in front of Minnie's stone. Touching the stone, he traces her name with his finger. "Mom. I'm home. I did all right and I'm glad it's over. I miss you. I wish you were here to help me know what to do with my life now that the war is over. All I thought about when I was over there was being back here. Now that I'm back, I don't know what to do with myself. It is all so different. I am so different." He pulls some weeds out from near the stone.

It is so peaceful in the cemetery. A few bird songs, the wind rustling the few remaining leaves on the maple trees, a passing car or two. Nothing else. No bullets whistling close by his head, no big guns pounding relentlessly, no anguished cries of comrades hit by enemy fire. He longs to stay in this peacefulness but knows he has another important call to make this day.

He promised himself that he would see Thomas Kersey's widow when he returned to the county. If a few words about her husband's service and how he died would give her some peace, then he wants to provide that. He wrote to her shortly after her husband's death, to tell her that her husband didn't suffer and to let her know that he would stop by after he returned home and they could have a longer conversation. Yesterday, he called her and made arrangements to visit with her today. He hopes that he hadn't sounded too crazy on the telephone; the stutter that he'd acquired during the war makes it hard to speak clearly, especially on the telephone to someone he doesn't know.

She gave him directions over the telephone, and it seems an easy address to find. He wonders how she is doing. Her husband had spoken so much about her and about his two young boys that he almost feels that he knows her. But then those conversations stopped with Kersey's death. Did his death change her at all? What about the boys? How were they doing? As he approaches Presque Isle, thinking these thoughts, once again he asks himself, 'Why not me? Why him? He had young children to raise. He was needed at home.'

He finds the street and the house is just as she'd described. He pulls into the driveway as she had said to do.

He puts out his cigarette, takes a deep breath, opens the car door, and walks to the front door. He doesn't have to knock. She is there.

"You must be Eddie. My husband wrote so much about you. Please come in."

He's glad that she's invited him into the kitchen where a fresh pot of coffee is brewing. He is most comfortable in women's kitchens, kitchens where mothers and grandmothers bake and bustle around. Over coffee, he tells her about her husband as a soldier and about his last day. "He didn't suffer at all. He was dead before he hit the ground. I don't think he even knew that he'd been hit." When she starts to cry, he passes her his handkerchief, unsure of what else to do. Comforting grieving widows is new territory for him. "Thank you so much for coming, Eddie. Your visit means so much to me," she tells him. They talk for a short time longer and then he gets up to leave. He doesn't expect that he will see her again. This visit has dredged up memories that he knows will now keep him awake for many nights. He wants to be done with memories.

Maybe it is time to look in at some of the used car lots. He will need a car if he expects to get himself to work once he finds something steady to do. That might be a good way to spend some of the rest of this day.

A Community Gives Thanks

On November 11, 1945, Veteran's Day, members of the Henry B. Pratt, Jr. Post of the American Legion in Caribou, local citizens, and other well-wishers, gather in the auditorium of Caribou High School to give thanks to Lieutenant Dahlgren for his courage in battle and for his efforts in defeating the German aggressors. The young lieutenant sits on stage with the local dignitaries who will give remarks during the program. His hands shake as he thinks about having to say a few words to the people who have come to honor him. He hopes he won't stammer too badly. He feels his jacket pocket for the slip of paper with the few lines he's written to say tonight.

Once everyone is seated, the Caribou High School band officially opens the program with a musical selection, followed by the invocation, a welcome from the chairman of the Caribou town council, and remarks from Brigadier General George Carter, the Adjutant General of the State of Maine. More music and then he hears his name. "And now, our guest of honor, Lieutenant Edward C. Dahlgren, of Woodland, Maine, recipient of the Congressional Medal of Honor, will say a few words."

The crowd stands and the applause is deafening. He almost wishes he were back at the front, just another soldier getting ready for the end of another day. He gets up from his seat and approaches the podium. He looks out at the crowd, and nods a sincere thank you and waits for the applause to end. He takes a deep breath and wishes for a cigarette and to be anywhere but here in the spotlight.

"Thhhhhhannnnk you. Thhhhhank you. I'm not much of ssssssspeaker but want you to knnnnnow how grateful I am thhhhhhhat you ccccccccame tonight." The stuttering will have to do. He can't control it. He looks out at his audience and gives them his trademark crooked smile, a gentle lift to the right, a smile so fleeting that you have to be looking for or will miss. He says just a few more words and returns to his seat.

The Reverend William Barnes of the Fort Fairfield Episcopal Church follows with an address that conveys the community's thanks "to the heroes from this area who fought and died so valiantly that justice and freedom might reign throughout the world."*(Aroostook Republican, 1945)* And the band follows with a spirited rendition of the National Anthem, sung by the entire audience.

During an informal reception at the close of the program, more than a thousand people come forward to shake Lieutenant Dahlgren's hand and to welcome him home. It is good to be home, and he vows that it will be a long time before he ever leaves home again.

Night Terrors

He stays with Viola for the fall and all of the winter. Wearing his army pants and an old jacket that Uncle John no longer needed, he works for area farmers throughout the winter in the potato houses, shoveling the stored potatoes into sacks for transport. It is familiar work, and he is tired at the end of the long days. Although she never asks for payment, every week he gives Viola money for his room and board.

He goes to bed early, sharing a room with his oldest cousin, Viola's son, Junior. Some nights, sleep comes easily but doesn't stay. During the nights, disturbing dreams lead to thrashing and yelling out in his sleep. Junior, awakened by his cousin's night terrors, seeks refuge in the living room and spends the remainder of many nights on the sofa.

Viola notices the changes in her cousin. He smokes continuously, finishing one cigarette only to light another. At the kitchen table, drinking coffee with her before leaving for work, his hands shake and he apologizes profusely when his unsteady hands spill coffee on the table. He stutters, especially when talking on the telephone. When his hands aren't occupied with a coffee cup or a cigarette, his fingers count out a cadence on the table. One, two, three, four...one, two, three, four. The cousin who returned from the war is very different from the easy going man she had known.

He never talks about what he experienced during the war, and when people ask him about his time in Europe, he simply replies, "It was tough and I'm glad to be home." Living with Viola and her family brings some recovery from the experiences of war. He enjoys the home-cooked meals and evening conversations. He gains some weight and starts to show an interest in being around other soldiers who had survived the war. He spends many Friday nights at local bars with other veterans, trying to drown out the memories only to awaken on Saturday with a pounding headache and all of his memories intact. He treasures the familiar routine of a dependable schedule and the quiet of Northern Maine. Rain gently tapping against a window, a train whistle announcing its arrival, the play-by-play of a baseball game on the radio are sounds that comfort.

Although Viola never suggests that he needs to find his own place, he feels that he is imposing on her. In order to live on his own, he needs to find work that is more dependable than the seasonal work he's found with area farmers. Army buddies from the 36th call and write, asking him when he is coming to Texas. "Eddie, there's plenty of work here. Come on down." He stutters a reply, "Maybe when ssssspring ccccomes." Truth be told, he has had enough of living in unfamiliar environments but can't tell his former buddies that he isn't coming. In time, they'll figure it out.

Thinking about the G.I. Bill 1946

At times in Europe, when he'd allow himself the luxury of thinking about a possible future back in the States, he and his buddies would speculate about life back home.

"I'm going back to Texas and buy the biggest and longest Buick ever made. What about you, Eddie? Why don't you come to Texas, too? You're almost a native by now!"

"I'll consider that a compliment coming from you, Pops. I'm not sure. I've been thinking, though, that I might like to be a civil engineer. I spent some time on a road crew and liked the idea of building new roads. Should be a lot of that kind of work once all the soldiers return home and buy cars and hit the roads."

Once home, he remembers those conversations. He knows that the G.I. Bill will pay for courses. He thinks he will talk with one of the fellows at the local American Legion. Surely one of them will have more information. He stops by the Legion post and makes arrangements to meet with the service officer who is in charge of helping vets with government programs. During that meeting, he finds out that, yes, the G.I. Bill will pay for courses and also give him a small living stipend. His new friend also knows that the only place in Maine where you can take courses to become an engineer is at the University of Maine in Orono.

Orono? That will mean another move, several hours south of Caribou. Where will he live? How will he survive four or more years of classes? He thinks back to his last experience thirteen years earlier when he was an undersized, country boy attending Caribou high school and feeling out of place. If he felt out of place then, how is he going to feel around college students? He is so restless, especially at night, still suffering from bruising nightmares, and the stuttering still hampers conversations. He's in no shape to sit for hours in classrooms, trying to learn complicated math formulas. He realizes that he is already twenty-nine years old, much older than other veterans who are considering college. And when and if he finishes? He'll be old at thirty-four and still not started with a career. He just can't wrap his head around a future four years down the road. He does well to simply get through each and every day. Discouraged and defeated before he even registers for his first course, he thinks that this dream of college is just that, a dream, a foolish pipe dream. Better put this idea permanently to rest, tuck it away in a box and file it on a high shelf in a closet, and get on with earning a living as best he can. Still, it is a disappointment.

A Room in Robinson

He returns to Viola's and tells her about his decision regarding college and his future. "I've got to find steady work and get myself out on my own."

When Viola's husband, Freddie, comes home that evening, he tells Eddie that he's seen an announcement at the post office that the State of Maine is going to be offering a test for potato inspectors and that veterans will be given extra points on their score. Freddie tells Eddie, "You could write to the Department of Agriculture in Augusta to schedule a time to take the test." Here is the possibility of a dependable income and an opportunity to establish independence.

He writes the letter, takes the test, and waits for the results. Several weeks later, a letter arrives, announcing that he had the top score on the test and that his veteran's points place him at the top of the registry. A job offer will surely follow.

A letter arrives soon after, offering a job covering an area in central Aroostook County, an area that includes Blaine, Bridgewater, Monticello, and Littleton. He'll have to find a place to live, but he now will have a job with a steady wage.

He packs his duffel and loads it into the second-hand Dodge that he bought a few weeks previously. "Viola. Thanks for everything. I'll come up in a couple of weekends, once I'm settled." He backs out of the driveway, looking over his shoulder, waving to Viola as he heads south.

He finds a room in a rooming house in Robinson, a place that isn't on the map but still a place that anyone in central Aroostook could tell you how to find. Situated alongside the Prestile Stream, this outpost has a general store, a gas station, a rooming house, and a popular fishing hole. His room is barebones simple: a bed and dresser, and a shared bathroom on the same floor as his rented room. Boarders have to fend for themselves for food. He can fry an egg and make toast but beyond that had always depended on his mother, his grandmother or the U.S. Army to provide for his meals. The local grocery is a source of canned goods so he's able to make do.

He quickly learns where all of the farmers in his district live and soon knows every farmer's name and reputation. He enjoys talking with these men who work the land and who have opinions about everything. He enjoys the predictable daily routine of driving to the area farms, walking up and down the rows of potatoes, and talking with the farmers. He finds common ground: discussing the prospects for a good harvest and speculating about the chances of the Red Sox for a winning season. The farmers like him, like his friendly ways and quick smile. Although they ask about where he comes from, he offers little information other than that he'd grown up just north of Caribou and had served in the Army during the war. Several of the people he meets suggest that he might want to join the local chapter of the American Legion.

Evenings during the summer and fall, he spends fishing along the banks of the Prestile Stream near his boarding house or he ventures farther afield to one of the area brooks. Most evenings he returns to his room with his limit of trout to present to his landlady.

He is getting by. Busy by day, still bothered at night by dreams of the past, he is grateful for life, something that many of his men were not privileged to have.

Fire and Ice, 1947

Edward Dahlgren and Pauline Mahan are members of the generation of the Great Depression and of World War II. As such, they have much in common: the potato farms, the long cold winters, the loss of loved ones.

Pauline Mahan is the only daughter of an Irish potato farmer. Until she finishes eighth grade, she grows up on Mouse Island, a settlement beside Mars Hill Mountain. The farm sits on the Canadian border and the consolidated school is a short walk up the road. Children who live too far to walk hitch a ride to school on a horse-drawn wagon. The summer immediately following her eighth-grade graduation, Pauline and family are dislodged from the farm. Although some Irish intrigue and family feuding likely came to a boil, the only fact that is known is that Uncle Bill took over the farm on Mouse Island, forcing Pauline's family to move several miles to another farm. She remembers walking with her mother along the dirt road behind the mountain, carrying a satchel of clothing, on their way to their next home. Four years later, in the spring just before her high school graduation, Pauline will lose her mother, Susan, who dies just a few weeks after an operation on her gall bladder.

She had wanted to be a secretary after she graduates from high school, but instead, she becomes an unpaid housekeeper for her bachelor brothers and widowed father. Day after day, they trek in potato dirt and she sweeps it back out. They eat her fresh bread and the eggs that she gathers each morning from under the hens. She hangs laundry out to dry on Monday mornings and irons the

Sunday shirts in the afternoon. Life is hard and she misses her mother's company.

In the summer of 1947, she is still hanging laundry and baking bread. A farmer's daughter with a beautiful milky complexion and lush brunette curls, Pauline catches the eye of the new potato inspector who comes to check the fields. He is still a thin rake whose war experience has left him with a stutter and a wariness about getting close to people. His icy blue eyes and shy demeanor appeal to her, and she makes it her job to draw him into conversation. She learns that he's from a small town near Caribou, that his mother died when he was in basic training, that he has been working in the potato houses near his uncle's home until just recently. This new job working for the State of Maine Department of Agriculture is a welcome change: steady pay and a chance to walk the potato fields alone with his thoughts. That is about all she learns about him; he never tells her about his war experience until years later when an occasional question might prompt a brief response.

He tells her that he's living in a rooming house in Robinson, a settlement so small as to not warrant a post office. He is lonely but used to it. He's learned during the war never to get too close to anyone. And he's learned from other life experiences that not only could war take your comrades, but that circumstance and illness could take your family.

They go out together on weekends and she introduces him to friends and relatives. They go dancing. She calls him at his rooming house and invites him to the farm for a home-cooked meal during the week. Her fire melts some of the ice in those blue eyes, and they marry on June 12, 1948.

A New Life 1948-49

He is a Protestant and she is a Catholic. In the late forties that means no church wedding. They ask two friends to stand up with them and make an appointment with a Justice of the Peace in Presque Isle, the city fifteen miles north of her home in Blaine. A simple ceremony, she in a beige suit, he in his robin's egg blue suit, they exchange vows. After the ceremony, they spend a night at a borrowed camp in E Plantation and then move their few belongings to a rented second floor apartment in Mars Hill.

Although he's told her he's been in the Army and spent time in Europe, he has not yet told her any of the details. She's found out early on in their relationship that if he doesn't want to talk about something that there will be no possibility of getting him to change his mind. When he sets his jaw forward, clamps his mouth tight, and looks at her with blue eyes gone to steel, she learns to change the subject. Now that they are married and will share a bed, he has to tell her about his frequent nightmares or risk scaring his new bride to death.

He has only one bedraggled suitcase with his clothes carefully folded inside. He's placed his uniform jackets on a hanger with a pillowcase cover to protect them from dust. He removes the pillowcase and starts to hang the coats in their bedroom closet. She notices the rows of ribbons.

"Tell me about those."

"Oh, I was in some pretty awful fights. I'd like to just forget about it all. I want you to know, though, that I'm sometimes restless at night. Don't want you to be frightened if I'm thrashing around."

Gradually he'll tell her more, even letting her know about his trip to Washington and about shaking President Truman's hand. He has pictures of the event. "President Truman told me that he'd much rather have that medal than be President of the United States." He chuckles. "I don't know if he really meant that or not."

He works, walking miles every day through the area potato fields, and she keeps the apartment spotless and cooks hearty hot meals. Occasionally they'll go dancing or to a movie on Saturday nights, sometimes in the company of another couple or two that she knows from having lived in the area all of her life. Life is quiet yet satisfyingly complete. She has a home of her own and he has stability, which includes a warm place to live and good meals. He is still troubled by nightmares which are especially bad when army buddies from the war call or write.

Several months after their marriage, she announces that she is pregnant. They'd talked about having children and are happy that a child is on the way, due to arrive in mid-July.

On the thirteenth of July, Eddie Dahlgren goes to work as usual but before he leaves, he asks his wife how she's feeling, knowing that the baby is due to arrive soon. She says she feels fine but is a bit tired. She thinks she won't do much housework today but will sit for a while in a comfortable chair and try to stay cool on this warm summer day. He says he'll try to get through with work a bit early.

When he comes home at noon for lunch, her back is aching and contractions have started. She feels she still has plenty of time before she needs to go to the local hospital, just a short distance away from their apartment. She waves him away. "Go back to work. I'll be fine."

By the time he finishes his stops for the day, a light rain has started falling. He opens the door to the apartment and she says, "I think we'd better go to the hospital." Her bag is packed. He picks it up and they head out.

At 5:30 p.m. on July 13, 1949, I was born: Susan Ruth Dahlgren, named for my mother's mother, Susan, and my dad's sister, Ruth.

*The East Room of the White House, Washington, DC. August 23, 1945.
The largest gathering of Medal of Honor recipients in the history of the
U.S. Lt. Dahlgren is sitting in front of President Harry S. Truman,
whose right hand rests on Dahlgren's shoulder.*

Lt. Edward C. Dahlgren receives his Medal of Honor from President Harry S. Truman

Lt. Edward C. Dahlgren, back home in Maine, recuperating at his sister's home in South Portland, 1945.

Pauline Cecilia Mahan, class of 1943, Aroostook Central Institute, Mars Hill, ME

Edward and Pauline Dahlgren, newly married in June of 1948.

Susan Ruth Dahlgren, born July 13, 1949 with her dad in the summer of 1950.

Just me and my dad, enjoying noon break outside on the steps, summer of 1951.

A Time for Everything

There is a time for everything,
And a season for every activity under the heavens:

A time to be born and a time to die,
A time to plant and a time to uproot,

A time to kill and a time to heal,
A time to tear down and a time to build,

A time to weep and a time to laugh,
A time to mourn and a time to dance,

A time to scatter stones and a time to gather them,
A time to embrace and a time to refrain from embracing,

A time to search and a time to give up,
A time to keep and a time to throw away,

A time to tear and a time to mend,
A time to be silent and a time to speak,

A time to love and a time to hate,
A time for war and a time for peace.

Ecclesiastes 3 (New International Version), 2010.

Chapter Five

Making the Most of It: the Post-War Years

What is it like to grow up in Northern Maine in the middle years of the twentieth century? What is it like to grow up with a dad who returns from World War II with a chest full of medals and a heart full of sorrow for the men he lead who are not coming home? What kind of man is this humble hero who just wants to forget the gruesome experiences of his war?

For the first twelve years of my life, I am unaware that Dad is anything other than just that—my dad. Although my siblings and I sometimes look at the medals he has tucked away in a dresser drawer, we instinctively ask no questions about their history. We know our father to be a hard worker who gets up every morning and drives out of our driveway on his way to inspect farmers' potato crops. Even when he is physically suffering from an attack of kidney stones, he gets up, goes to work and eventually comes home. His regularity is a predictable and comforting part of growing up. We know that he is very involved with the local American Legion, serving as commander and service officer for many terms. Somehow we know that this organization is important to him. And, on patriotic holidays such as Memorial Day and the Fourth of July, we sit on the hood of our car, awaiting the parade and our dad who will be marching in the front with his Legion buddies.

Dad is not demonstrative, like most men of his generation. Though we don't hear him telling us that he loves us, on some deep level, we are each confident that we are the most important aspects of our father's life. As the oldest of the Dahlgren children, I am lucky to have Dad in my life for 57 years.

As I remember him, it's a challenge to capture the essence of my time with Dad; there is just so much that can be included. From the time he pushes me off and away from the kitchen steps and I take my first few wobbly turns on my new bicycle, to Dad shaking my hand at my high school graduation, to him holding my son Matthew, dressed in his baptism outfit, complete with ruffled hat, Dad is always someone I want to be with. I never think I'll ever lose him, but the end does come and with it, the end of creating memories together. Now, I can only look back at what I had and conclude that I wouldn't change one single thing about my growing up in a small town in Northern Maine in the shadow of Mars Hill Mountain.

I am the first of the babies to join the Dahlgren household, born in 1949, a bona fide "Baby Boomer." Pictures of me as an infant, cradled in Dad's arms or perched securely on Mom's lap, chronicle an early life of being protected and cared for by parents who welcomed me into their world. This is postwar America. Returning soldiers are anxious to settle down to the business of raising families and succeeding in jobs. It's a simpler time, when dads go to work and moms stay home. On the surface, my childhood might appear as idyllic. Yet, now with the perspective gained from age, I am aware of the shadows that lurked just under the surface for Dad, shadows that came home with him from the war.

Dad goes to work every day. Employed by the State of Maine Department of Agriculture as a potato inspector, Dad's responsibilities change with the seasons. In the summer when the potato crops are growing, he walks row on row through the fields, checking for disease and for the percentage of varietal mixture. So as not to contaminate one field with the problems of a previous field, he dips his work boots in a coal tar disinfectant solution before stepping into a new field. He stops to chat with farmers, giving them his report about how their crops are doing. Although he is sometimes the bearer of bad news, that a farmer's crops are not healthy enough to be certified as seed for the next season, he is popular and well-liked. I believe he enjoys his job: he's his own boss for the most part and the familiar routine of what he does provides a structure to his days that is most welcome. He sets his own work schedule and all the walking is a balm for his troubled soul. He never again wants to be responsible for another man's life. This job provides a steady paycheck for a growing family, a job that comes with few demands. If he's inspecting fields close by, he'll come home for his lunch. If not, Mom packs his black dinner bucket with sandwiches and sweets. He is always home for supper, tired after a day of walking field upon field, ever thankful for a home-cooked meal and a family.

And Mom stays home. Home is a modest, single-story ranch on Route 1, built with a V.A. loan. In 1950, Route 1, the principal road in and out of Central and Northern Maine, is still a dirt road. Dad, who never liked to borrow money, would probably not have ventured into home ownership if not for Mom's urging. For both, this home is a castle, albeit a one-level, brand-spanking new castle with central heat and running water. For two people who grew up having to draw well water, use outdoor toilets, and work a woodpile season after season, having such a home is an undreamed of luxury. The house they build together they will live in together until Dad's death.

Our home faces the mountain. Looking out the kitchen window at the mountain often provides us with a pretty accurate weather forecast. When the mountain takes on a somber blue cast with a thick blanket of clouds overhead, a storm is likely. When the sun shines, we live in the shadow of our mountain.

When I recall my childhood, so many times I'm drawn to memories of supper around the oak table which Mom bought second-hand from a neighbor. The claw-footed table from the turn of the twentieth century has two leaves so it can accommodate the six of us sitting around it for the evening meal.

And what meals they are! At the heart of our parents' care for us is that we always have enough to eat and are always warm in the winter. Everything else is a luxury. Potatoes are central to every main meal, as are home-made desserts. Having survived the sugar rationing of the war years, Mom loves the abundant supply of sugar available again to her for making apple pie, chocolate cake, and molasses cookies. Her cooking leads to four children always on the chubby side of normal.

By the time I turn seven, I have three younger siblings. Brian and Mike, just thirteen months apart, are all but twins and provide constant company for each other. I am somewhat left alone, being the oldest, so turn to solitary amusements such as reading. When Mom announces in the fall of 1955 that we are going to have a new baby brother or sister in June, I secretly hope for a little sister.

Judy arrives on June 2, 1956, a pretty little blond, and I quickly realize that this baby will have to grow a lot in order to be much of a companion for me. I go back to my books and my dolls.

When Judy is a few months old, she starts fussing when left alone for her nap in the afternoons. On weekends, I dutifully sit beside her crib until she goes to sleep. When the fussiness doesn't stop and when it becomes apparent that Judy isn't responding to family members' voices, Mom makes an appointment with the local doctor. Although born without any hearing problems, Judy is now severely hearing impaired. The doctor speculates that the hearing loss might be due to German measles, rampant in the community this past summer. He explains that sometimes people don't even know they have the measles but that a case in an infant can certainly cause such hearing loss.

Other than places to buy a hearing aid, there are no services for hearing impaired children at this time in Northern Maine. Two resources are available down state, one at the University of Maine in Orono and another at a hospital in Waterville, and there's also the Baxter School for the Deaf in the Portland area where Judy can be instructed in sign language. "No," says Mom to this last idea. "Judy is going to learn to speak and go to school here. I don't want her living away from home." Dad agrees and for the next several years, they make many trips to the resources in Orono and Waterville where Judy receives speech therapy. Even with their limited income, our parents find ways to be even more frugal so that Judy gets the help she needs.

And, no matter the cost, the Dahlgren family will stay intact. In the little house in Blaine, two boys to a bedroom and two girls to another, we grow up secure in the knowledge that our parents will take good care of us. We don't have vacations away from home or summer camp experiences, but we have much more: the experience of growing up with parents committed to giving us a solid foundation in values that will serve us all well as adults.

As an adult looking back at my childhood, I also realize that my parents keep us innocently unaware of serious issues, such as Dad's continued problems with war memories. Mom knows about his restlessness at night and about his use of over-the-counter sleep and pain remedies. She knows about his bouts of drinking during card games with Legion buddies. She doesn't allow liquor in our home which, in retrospect, provides Dad with a level of control over alcohol. She hears him stuttering on the telephone when he makes his obligatory calls to farmers and wishes she could do this part of his job for him. She sees his hands shake and feels that there are moments when he is somewhere else other than in Blaine, Maine. And she knows about his emotional distancing, about how he will lose himself in a ballgame on the radio in the evening rather than spend time with her and the children. For the most part, she doesn't complain. He's a good man, a good provider, and a good father. And, as the years pass, creating a distance from the war, it seems that the responsibilities of raising a family, keeping a job, and eventually participating in many community activities help him to put the memories of war in the shadows.

> *"The first winter after the war I wasn't feeling good. Then the first thing you know I got married and started having kids right away. Before I knew it I had a flock of youngsters. It's a lot to think about before picking up and moving out, right? Have to have something to eat, to wear. It's probably just as well. There's a lot worse places to live than here. Leastways we don't have much crime. It could be worse. Could be a lot worse."* (Edward Dahlgren, interview for *Yankee Magazine*, September, 1981, p. 202).

In the first few years after the war ends, his buddies from Texas call and write regularly, inviting him to come on down. Work is plentiful and they miss him. He stalls, putting them off, telling them that maybe sometime in the future, he'll be down. He just doesn't know how relocating a family is possible. It just seems like too much to take on. By 1956 when there are four children in the household and several years of seniority with his job, he feels like settling. Aroostook County is home, a place he knows, a place where he feels safe. Eventually, the fellows from Texas stop calling. They accept that Eddie will not be coming down any time soon.

During these early years of my childhood, I am unaware of the skill it had to have taken my parents to provide for such a large family. For several years, they find a way to feed and clothe a family of six on an income of $67.00 per week. They are frugal to be sure—Yankee frugal. Mom clips coupons to take with her when she shops for groceries. A large vegetable garden that they plant together every spring yields many quarts of canned beans, carrots, and peas. Shelves in our basement are full of jars of pickles: bread and butter pickles, pickled beets, green tomato pickles, and mustard pickles. Mom makes jams from native chokecherries and wild cranberries that we help her gather from bushes growing along the farm roads. Potatoes are always free for the asking, and Dad brings buckets-full home on a weekly basis. Mom bakes all of the desserts from scratch and makes bread weekly. We are never hungry but every so often supper is fried bologna or Spam with several sides of homegrown vegetables.

Both of our parents have survived the Depression and know well how to live within their means. Dad in particular is loathe to buy anything "on time," the sixties term for making monthly payments for purchases. At times when an appliance up and dies, he has to give in and finance a replacement. For example, when Mom's wringer washer bites the dust, a new and improved automatic washer comes into our lives. They pray that nothing else breaks before this expense is paid off.

As my siblings and I each approach high school age, we are able to help out with our own expenses, such as buying school clothes by working during the potato harvests. In the 1960s when potatoes are the mainstay of the Northern Maine economy, there isn't any able-bodied teenager who doesn't work in the fields during September and into October.

Dad's job provides us with a steady income and a new car every three years. After that first second-hand Dodge that he bought when he started working for the state, he switches his allegiance to Chevrolets. A new car is one of Dad's few indulgences; he reasons that he needs reliable transportation in order to do his job.

When it's time for a trade, he and Mom drive to Presque Isle to wrangle with the car salesman for the best deal. She offers ideas on the color scheme, but he selects other features such as engine size. In the days of cheap gas, a V8 engine is the preferred choice. In the early sixties, the new cars are two-toned beauties with fins and luxurious upholstery. In the evenings after Dad gets home from work and we've had supper, we often all pile in the car and go for a ride around the back roads. Sometimes we stop at the local Dairy Freeze for cones of soft-serve ice cream. On nights when a bit more money is available, we have milkshakes or sundaes. "Get what you'd like" is the password for extravagance.

It's not until I go to college in Boston in the fall of 1967 that I realize that other people have a lot more material goods and worldly experience than I. My roommates and classmates talk about vacations on the Maine coast and ask if I live anywhere near the sandy beaches. Not only is my home in Northern Maine a long seven hours from these beaches, but I've never even been to the places they talk about. Growing up, we'd never taken vacations. We are simply off from school for the summer and make the most of it. We are not unlike the majority of all the families in our community. Maybe the potato farmers buy a new car or pick-up truck sooner than the rest of us, but mostly we all have about the same.

We don't have music lessons or weeks at summer camp. We do have Sunday picnics where the whole family, all six of us, piles into the Chevrolet and heads for a cool spot to have a lunch. Mom packs the wooden picnic basket with homemade potato salad, hotdogs and hamburgers, and a homemade desert. A two gallon metal cooler holds Kool-Aid. Dad always drives and even though he's been driving all week and might like to spend a Sunday at home listening to a Red Sox game on the radio, he always comes with us on these picnics. When Judy is small, she sits in front between Mom and Dad in what today would be an unacceptable booster seat. Brian, Mike, and I would squabble over who got to sit in the middle in back, the worst seat in the house.

We have encyclopedias, two sets of these wonders of the world, in fact. What knowledge they contain! We have library cards and are encouraged to read. Magazines and newspapers are always available at our house. I remember from my earliest days at home with my parents their ritual at the breakfast table of passing each other sections of the *Bangor Daily News*, the daily paper that's delivered at the end of our driveway very early every morning.

From the time each of us starts our school careers, we know fully how much our parents value education. For Mom, "an education is something they can't take away from you." And for Dad, it's something that he didn't get to complete. They join the P.T.A. and Dad serves as a School Board member for many years. Our papers and report cards are reviewed with praise and posted on the refrigerator. There is never a question in our household about our futures: we will each attend college. And together always, both of our parents attend all of our graduations, proud of our accomplishments. I owe so much to them.

In sum, growing up with Dad, we know him to be a great guy who works hard and always takes an interest in anything that the four of us are doing. We grow up knowing that he's a veteran of World War II and proudly watch him march with his Legionnaire buddies in the local parades on Memorial Day. We've seen the drawer-full of medals but never can get him to say but a word or two about how he earned them. The one that attracts our interest the most is the one that's attached to a pale blue

ribbon with a field of stars on the portion that holds the
medal.

In June of 1963, we will learn that this medal and our
dad are rather special to the world beyond us. Because of
having received this medal—the Medal of Honor, for
extraordinary bravery during World War II—he is to be the
guest of honor at Loring Air Force Base's Armed Forces
Day. Loring AFB, located in Limestone, Maine, some thirty
miles north of us, is the largest SAC base east of the
Mississippi at the time. With its full complement of B52
bombers and nuclear warheads, it's known to us because
of the daily fly-bys that lead us to look skyward. We have
never visited the base; all are excited about the prospect of
a day's adventure.

In preparation for the day, Mom buys white shirts,
dress slacks, and bow ties for Brian and Mike. Dad's one
and only suit goes out to the dry cleaners for a pressing.
And, Mom, ever frugal when it comes to buying anything
for herself, splurges for this special day and finds a classy
beige suit and a Jackie Kennedy pillbox hat for the
occasion.

We are to be picked up by an Air Force officer and
driven to the base for the ceremony. Imagine our
excitement about riding in an official government vehicle!
We are starting to realize that maybe our Dad's someone
quite special.

The ceremonies of the day begin with a parade lead by
the Royal Canadian Dragoon's drum and bugle corps. On
the reviewing stand with base commander Colonel W.H.
Reddell and other dignitaries, is our dad, the beribboned
Medal of Honor around his neck. As participants in the
parade pass the reviewing stand, all give snappy salutes as
they pass by Dad.

We are treated like royalty for the day. Lunch is at the
officer's club where the colonel and his wife are the
gracious hosts. After lunch, we tour the base, escorted by
the base commander. Brian and Mike even get to try out
fighter pilot helmets for fit. A picture from the day shows
them needing to grow a bit more in order to sign up for
service. Throughout the day's events, civilian groups
touring the base glance our way, perhaps wondering who

the handsome man in the civilian suit is who is being treated to such honors.

Like all events, this one comes to an end, though, with a return escort back home. It's an especially sweet return since the thoughtful colonel's wife has made sure that a large bakery box full of frosted cinnamon buns found its way into the back seat of the station wagon.

Once home, we quickly change into jeans and shorts. Dad hangs up his suit and puts on his well-worn khakis and a plaid shirt. Mom puts away her dressy outfit, gets out her apron and begins the process of preparing a supper for a soon-to-be hungry family. The Cinderella day is over and life quickly returns to normal in our household.

Let it be said that my dad is much more than a collection of issues brought home from the war and most of my memories of growing up with Dad are happy memories, involving every-day, perfectly ordinary happenings, occasions as simple as shelling peas together in early July.

In addition to the ubiquitous potato fields, peas are planted as the second cash crop in Aroostook. Because of Dad's relationships with area farmers, he's often invited to take all the peas he can carry from the fields. The peas come home in bunches, pods and vines intertwined. Since Dad brings them home, Mom makes it clear that he can deal with shelling them. The division of labor is clearly demarked in our household. She deals with anything internal to the house—she'll freeze the shelled peas; he's to take care of anything and everything beyond the kitchen door.

About the time I turn twelve, and on through adulthood, I am Dad's pea-shelling helper. Each year just before the Fourth of July holiday, we set up business in the double bay garage, intent on getting the entire mess of peas shelled before the end of the day. With the garage doors open and a refreshing breeze blowing towards us, we both look forward to a pleasant few hours together. The system takes some time to set up: two aluminum lawn chairs, two buckets for peas to be shelled, two bowls for the newly shelled peas, and several bags for discarded shells. Dad is in charge of the placement of equipment. I just need to stay out of the way.

Okay. All set. Go! Seated in the lawn chairs each with a bowl in our laps and a bucket of peas to be shelled on the floor close by, we start the process.

For novices to pea shelling, there is one correct and many incorrect ways to shell peas. This I learn from Dad. If you want to make the process go quickly and efficiently, then you need to hold the pod so that the seam is facing up. Press firmly with your thumb on the end of the pod that is not the end that grew on the vine. Pop! The pod opens and tender baby peas line up in a row awaiting release. Again, a thumb works best to push the peas out of the pod and into the bowls. Ting, ting, ting, tang go the peas as they tumble into the metal bowls.

We work contentedly, side by side, watching the traffic go by on Route 1. Throughout the morning, Dad stops shelling long enough to wave to drivers passing by. Once in a while, we eat a few of the raw, fresh peas just released from their captivity. We talk about whatever happens to cross our minds or we sit silently with only the music of the peas interrupting the quiet. I have that kind of relationship with Dad, where we can simply be together without conversation. I enjoy the peace that comes with these simple times, shelling peas, talking or not, just coexisting and being content with each other's company. To this day, the only peas I like to eat are the raw, fresh peas from a pod, peas that never fail to remind me of these special times with my father.

My brothers, on the other hand, have memories of going fishing with Dad. In the spring as April moves into May and farmers start turning the ground to ready it for planting, the swift streams swollen by winter snow melt have settled down enough to chance flipping a fishing line into the water. Dad knows all the best spots. This knowledge is a byproduct of his work, walking the potato fields and observing the streams and brooks that create the borders for many fields. I am not terribly fond of earthworms, Dad's favorite bait, so I never catch the fishing bug. Brother Brian, though, loves going with Dad.

To prepare for a few hours of fishing Three Brooks, Dad heads to any one of a number of farmers' barns where right next to the barns' foundations—where heat rises from manure piles, fresh earthworms are large and plentiful. Dad has a special metal container, made for the purpose of transporting bait. He digs a hole in the manure-enriched dirt, puts some loose dirt in his container, then sets to work finding earthworms, which he drops into their home away from home. He closes the lid of the worm can. Then he and Brian are ready to see how the fish are biting. Brook trout is his game and he is terribly good at catching his limit. And we are equally good at finishing off the fresh fish, fried to perfection in Mom's cast iron pan.

Dad loves to fish for brook trout and knows all of the most lucrative spots in the area or so it seems to us. Whenever he comes back from an afternoon of fishing, we know we will have a pan full of delicious fried brook trout for supper...but not before Mom finishes the ugly job of gutting and cleaning the fish. She grumbles over the job and to this day, I don't know how that division of labor came about. I can only assume it must have had something to do with man bringing home the bacon and the wife cooking it. Once the fish are cleaned, she dredges each one through salted flour and puts them in the cast iron frying pan with bubbling oil. The trout sizzle and turn crisp on the outside, tender sweet on the inside. A second frying pan sputtering with home-fried potatoes and another pot boiling with fresh peas rounds out the meal.

Dad's secret to catching fish doesn't have anything to do with expensive, fancy equipment. Rather, it has everything to do with patience. With a can of worms, a few hooks, and a weathered reel, he simply out-waits the fish. Dad's patience and self-control are definite virtues on one particular fishing excursion where he and Brian almost catch more than they counted on: they nearly drown in one of the local streams...

Recent rains had raised the water level in all of the area brooks. Where shallow waters with a few waist high pools had once described the brooks, now the depth of the water is an unknown. Keeping this uncertainty in mind, Dad and Brian wade carefully away from the shore.

With fresh earthworms secured on their rods, they each cast out their lines and wait. Not so patient, though, are the black flies, a byproduct of the recent rains. Covered in a thick application of Old Woodsman fly dope, Dad and Brian are somewhat protected from the onslaught of the bane of northern New England, black flies. Still, the flies dart around their heads and keep up a steady attack. "Did you feel a tug there on your line?"

"Nope, how about you?"

"Guess not. Let's go out a little further."

They walk slowly out towards the center of the stream. The current is swift and the water is cooler than what is to be expected at this time of year. Brian takes a short step forward and sinks up to his shoulders. He's found a pool of high water, deeper than he wants. For a non-swimmer like Dad, this much water beneath him is enough to make him frightened of drowning. He freezes, not daring to step back or forward.

Dad is just two steps behind Brian. "Brian, don't worry. We'll be okay. We'll get out of this. Just stay there. I'm coming. I'll get you."

Only a couple of inches taller than Brian, Dad is not at much of an advantage in the fast current. But, he said that they'll be okay and Brian believes in Dad. Dad walks carefully forward, reaches out his hand to Brian, who grabs the extended arm and slowly, one careful step at a time, the two make their way back to more shallow water.

They continue to fish, side by side, and with patience catch their limit that day. But more than the day's catch that came home for supper, the afternoon's near tragedy deepens Brian's respect for our father who is, from that day forward, in Brian's words, "the bravest man I ever knew."

Another summer experience that Dad enjoys, as I've mentioned, involves attending the harness racing at the Presque Isle fairgrounds. And a highlight of the summer for my siblings and me is the week during July when not only are the horses running but the Northern Maine Fair is in full swing. Every year, we wait anxiously for Dad to come home so we can spend an afternoon enjoying the Tilt-a-Whirl, the Ferris Wheel, and other rides. Cotton candy, frozen ice cream treats on a stick, and candy apples all vie for our attention. Mom enjoys Bingo and Dad enjoys the afternoon horse races.

From his earliest days as a youngster, spending time with his uncles on their farms, hanging out in their barns grooming the horses, Dad enjoys everything about horses. Although the fair itself lasts just one short week, the racing season in Northern Maine stretches through several weeks of the summer. The races are in the evenings with an occasional afternoon lineup added during fair week. Sometimes one of my siblings or I go with Dad to the races; on other evenings, he goes with some of his friends who also enjoy the races. I remember especially well the MacDonald brothers from Bridgewater who always stopped in to pick up Dad on their way by.

A beep on the horn would announce their arrival followed by a "Hi, Ed." Bernard always gets out of the front seat so that Dad can sit up front. In Bernard's world, guests are offered the best seat in the house. There are no finer men in Dad's life than Buzz and Bernard MacDonald. Devout Catholics, they are in church every Sunday and every holy day. When they approach any Catholic church on their way to the races, they all make the sign of the cross in complete reverence. Silently they each say a prayer. "If it please you, God, let us win tonight so that we can make a bigger contribution to the collection basket at Sunday mass."

Sometimes I go with Dad to the races and we find some of his friends to sit with. Before the first race starts, Dad studies the program which lists all of the recent statistics on horses and drivers. "What do you think, Susie? Does this one have a chance?" I don't know the first thing about horse races but Dad teaches me what to look at in the numbers. "This one's due for a win. Look at the times she finished recently. How about a two dollar bet on this one?" His mind made up, Dad steps down from the grandstand

and walks over to the betting booth. He places his bet and returns to his seat.

Before we can count to ten, the horses and their drivers, clad in bright racing silks, sitting astride their two-wheeled sulkies, line up behind the starting car. The car takes off, horses following behind. "They're off!" yells the announcer. The car speeds up and races off the track, clearing the way for the horses. Two times around the track the horses go, kicking up clods of dirt and spreading dust over everything. "Damsel's coming up fast. Here comes Rust Bucket. It's neck and neck! There she goes. It's Damsel in the lead..." We stand up with the crowd, yelling, "Come on, Damsel!!" Dad and I are into it, cheering with the rest of the crowd. "And the winner by a neck is—Damsel!" We clap and clap. This is our horse and she's not the odds-on favorite so Dad's happy. Winning twenty dollars, we're up by eighteen.

And on it goes for the next eight races of the evening. We eat steamed hot dogs, drink cold Cokes in paper cups, and watch the sun go down and the lights come up. It's great fun to be with Dad.

Because he never has much money to spend on the horse races, he is very careful with his bets and most nights, betting on the horses or playing cards with his buddies, he generally comes home ahead of the game. If on the rare night he comes home in the hole, he will only admit to 'breaking even,' the code for not having a successful outing. At the end of one memorable outing in 1959, he comes home, not with extra money in his pocket, but with a car for Mom. Here's the story.

Because our one car is Dad's portable office, Mom is left without transportation during the weekdays. We live half a mile from the small Mom & Pop store where you can walk to for a loaf of bread or gallon of milk at inflated prices, and pick out several pieces of penny candy with the change that's left over. The larger grocery stores, Newberry's, the bank, and other sundry shops are a mile away, which is deemed much too far to walk and carry back items. Mom frequently bemoans the fact that she's stuck without a car—and stuck with us all day to boot! Her complaints come to an end one morning when she looks out the kitchen window to see parked on the rise of lawn just beyond the driveway, a genuine Woodie station wagon! "Where did that come from?"

Dad had returned late from a card game the night before and the 1952 Woodie came along with him. "I bought it from Jake Lawrence."

"It looks like a piece of junk. How much did you pay for that thing?"

"I got a good deal on it." That's as far as he's going with a reply. In all likelihood, he'd won it from Jake. Dad usually came away from card games the winner.

Out we go to inspect our new gem. Yes, the Woodie's a senior citizen and showing her age. Rust falls off her sides as we open the doors. The interior isn't much better: the seats are split and springs peek out when Mom sits down. "Ouch! I think this thing bit me."

"Start her up and see how she sounds," Dad encourages her. She steps on the clutch and pushes in on the start button. We hear some grinding and complaining from the engine and then a roar like a rocket taking off as all systems connect. Black smoke comes out the exhaust. "I think she had a little gas," Dad quips.

"I can't drive this thing. I can't see over the steering wheel. And the seat—does it move any farther forward?" Mom's all of five feet tall. Accommodations will have to be made if she's to see where she's going in this rig. She gets out and Dad hops in, hoping to be able to adjust the seat forward. He finds a lever, pulls, and the seat rushes forward to the steering wheel, jailing him in. He pulls the lever again, gently this time, and moves the seat back a bit.

"There. That should do it. Now, get a pillow and you'll be all set. Take her for a ride if you'd like." Mom climbs back in, then looks to us kids to join her.

I'm of the age where being embarrassed is what I try to avoid at all costs—and being seen in this junk box would be a huge source of embarrassment. I swallow my pride, however, and skulk into the backseat, slamming the door behind me. My siblings, on the other hand, are excited about this new addition to the family and can't wait to hit the road. These are the days before seatbelts and toddler seats so I just settle baby sister Judy close to me in the backseat.

Mom gives the beast gas and lurches forward. Even before we've left the driveway, the door on my side flies open. "Hold on, Mom. The door isn't shut," I tell her. I reach over and slam the door for a second time. It must weigh a hundred pounds. Cars were built with lots of steel in those days. Mom tries a second time. The engine roars—and the door flies open again. "What a piece of junk!" she declares.

Eventually, though, the door stays shut and we are off on our maiden voyage, with me hoping that none of my friends are outside as we pass by. As it is, the seat is so low that just the top of my head is visible so I would have been safe from stares. We drive around some of the farm roads and then turn back for home. A fifteen-minute first run is a long enough gamble. Nellie Bell does just fine.

Nellie Bell will see us through several seasons and over time, Mom comes to appreciate the luxury of having transportation, regardless of the rust, the backfiring and the doors that don't always stay closed. When Judy is old enough to bring to the potato fields during harvest, Mom loads Nellie Bell with lunches and the aluminum picnic Kool Aid jug and drives her crew of migrant workers to her brother's farm.

No story about my dad would be complete if it didn't contain a reference to his love of baseball and the Boston Red Sox. Growing up in Northern Maine where true spring never comes in mid-March but might be with us to stay by the middle of May, the predictable strains of "Play Ball!" coming from Dad's radio in April lets us know that spring has truly arrived somewhere in the country. Somewhere in the United States, there's no snow on the ground. Somewhere there's green grass and a pitcher on a mound tossing a white ball, intent on winning this outing for his team.

Dad loves the game of baseball—not as much as he loves all of us, but I do have to believe that baseball does come in a very close second on his list. When he is just a youngster growing up in the Swedish communities of Northern Maine, a game of baseball during school recess makes his day. Later as a young adult in the 1930s, he plays on one of the many town teams cropping up across Aroostook County. Legend has it that he had a strong arm and a good eye for hitting the ball into the outfield. In August of 1945, he is in Washington D.C. awaiting a meeting with President Truman and spends many hot and humid afternoons watching Washington's major league baseball team. It must have seemed all a dream to him as he sat in the stands listening intently to the crack of a bat. And once he is truly home, back in Northern Maine, it is the radio broadcasts of the Red Sox games which momentarily help him to forget the war that haunts him still.

When I remember Dad and springtime in Northern Maine, it seems like it's just yesterday, hearing his commentary on the radio commentary about the game.

"Ball four!" yells out the announcer, followed by Dad's response: "Damn. Get that pitcher off the mound," yells Dad. "He's not a bit of good. He's going to lose the game."

His running commentary carries into the kitchen from the breezeway connecting the house to the garage where he listens to the Red Sox game, an ash tray on the arm of the chair he sits in, set in just the right place for flicking the ashes off his ever-present filterless Camel. An armchair athlete for years now, he knows the game well. No fan has more heart for his team than Dad for the boys from Boston.

"How are they doing?" One or another of us peeks around the kitchen counter for an update. If the Sox are winning, a big, lopsided grin accompanies the reply.

"They're ahead by one run but the big hitters are coming up for the Yankees. The Sox need to can this pitcher or they'll lose the game." Despite the fact that he has to get up early in the morning and head out for the potato fields, he listens to the entire game, even if it goes into extra innings. If the Sox lose, we hear him declare, "They're not a darn bit of good. That's it. I don't think I'm going to listen to any more games this season." True to his word, he might skip a night or two, but his love of the game will always outlive the Red Sox record and before we can say, "Strike three. You're out!" he's back to his favorite evening spot with the radio tuned in to the station carrying the game.

Although he never plays baseball again after he comes home from the war, Dad passes on his skills to each of us, playing hours of catch with us on the front lawn. My brothers both benefit from his instruction—each plays baseball for our high school. I, on the other hand, am a hopeless case. Dad praises me when I catch the ball in the pocket of brother Michael's left-handed glove but has little to say about my toss back to him. I can catch well enough, but I have no throwing arm. My baseball career is limited to some pickup softball games during grammar school recesses.

As the years go on, the four of us leave home, only to return for frequent visits, and if it's baseball season, we enjoy talking with Dad about his team. Sometimes of an evening, we watch the game with him, now that he has his very own television set dedicated to his sports viewing. His TV set and a comfortable padded rocker with a warm blanket resting on the chair's back are arranged in the bedroom that used to be mine. When I come to visit, if it is during baseball season, he'll excuse himself from conversations in the living room, announcing that he guesses he'll go check on how the Sox are doing. Before heading into the bedroom, he trots off to the kitchen for supplies: a handful of sugar free cookies and paper towels to catch the crumbs. Periodically throughout the evening, he'll return to the living room to give us an update on the game and to raid the cookie jar one more time. And, throughout the evening, I'll peek into the bedroom and watch a bit of the game over his shoulder.

What I wouldn't give for more of these moments. With Dad's death in May of 2006, his television set falls quiet. Never a huge sports fan growing up, I become a rabid Red Sox fan with Dad's death. It is one of my ways of keeping him close. As I sit on my sofa in my living room, listening to the last game of the season of 2006, listening to the Sox beat the Yankees for one last time, I picture that signature crooked grin on Dad's face. He'd have loved it. Even though his team isn't going to the World Series this year, at the very least, they end their season beating the Yankees.

In addition to baseball, Dad loves to play cards: poker, cribbage, hearts...the game doesn't matter but the winning does. He grows up playing cards with his Swedish aunts and uncles around the kitchen table on weekends. A card game is an excuse to visit and doesn't cost anything, unless the players are betting, which didn't happen in Mama Minnie's household. Later when he plays with his buddies, a little money on the table just seems to sweeten the event, and he's such a good card player, he usually wins regardless of the game. On the rare occasion when he isn't winning, his displeasure is noticeable in his voice, in his blue eyes that turn to ice and look right through the other players, in his pointed index finger advising the dealer to hurry it along. Each of us learns to play cards from him and as my brothers grow up, they often play with Dad. Mike remembers one particular game that ended badly for Dad. Here's the story in my brother Michael's words...

"It's early June and we are on a fishing trip on Beaver Brook near Escourt, way up north in the Maine woods. Ralph Foster, who's the immigration supervisor at Madawaska before I started working there, owns the camp and lets us borrow it during our trip. It's evening and rather cool so I build a fire in the wood stove. While we're waiting for the others to get back to camp, Dad and I decide to play cribbage. To say that the game isn't going well for Dad is an understatement. I end up "double skunking" him, which for someone of Dad's skill is unheard of. To get double skunked at cribbage, you have to score less than 60 points of a total number of 120 points. Dad's so mad at losing the game that he throws the cribbage board in the wood stove where it catches fire. Because the board belongs to Ralph Foster, I make sure that I replace it before Ralph finds out. Otherwise, we'd be out of luck with borrowing his camp in the future!"

On the other hand, when Dad's winning at cards, he's all smiles. Another story involves a foursome at our kitchen table. Dad, Brian, Mike, and our Uncle Mac play hearts many nights for hours on end. As nonplussed as Dad is at most things in life, Uncle Mac is just the opposite. Uncle Mac's temper can flare at nothing or everything. Like our dad, Mac also hates to lose at cards. Unlike Dad, Mac isn't as often the victor, so he's often in a temper.

On this particular evening, Mike and Dad each win three of four games of hearts when Mac "starts bitching about the fairness of the game." Mac spouts out, "You all play right a'gin me!"—one of his stock lines when he isn't doing well. Even though he's accusing the others of not playing fairly, Uncle Mac would never think of quitting in the middle of a nightly challenge. As the next round finishes with Dad winning, Dad asks, "Where did Mac finish?" Brian answers that Mac finished third (which of course is as bad as finishing last). Dad says, 'Well, that's pretty good," in his best teasing yet smug voice. It, to put it mildly, is not well received by Mac.

Prior to the war, he enjoyed the sport of hunting. "Eddie Dahlgren was always a good shot, good enough to shoot the heads off two partridges one after the other with a . 30-.30." (Allen, 1981, 192). After the war, he likes to be out with friends at camp but takes no pleasure in killing animals, even if it means extra meat on the table for his family. He hunts for the camaraderie, for the time to be with other men, playing cards during the evenings and walking through the woods all day.

When Mike is in high school in the early seventies, he and Dad sometimes hunt together. They go down to Uncle Mac's farm and walk the fields and woods behind the farm house. Some seasons they see deer but not always. One particular time they spot a deer and Dad, who see it first, gets a shot off. He sees the bullet hit the deer in the midsection, below where he expects the shot to land. The deer stumbles but doesn't fall. "A gut shot. The worst kind. We've got to find the poor thing," says Dad. They track the deer until dusk but find nothing but a few drops of blood.

It's too dark to do anything more. "Did you hear that deer cry? Sounded just like a baby."

Father and son walk out of the woods. No words are exchanged, but Mike knows by observing Dad shaking his head that he feels terrible about the deer, terrible and helpless to do anything to ease the creature's suffering. Once at the car, they check their rifles, emptying the bullets, putting the safeties on. "You drive, Mike," he says, still too shaken to want to get behind the wheel to drive home.

This is the last time Dad ever goes into the woods to hunt for deer. Although we know through his telling of this story that the episode bothers him, I don't believe any of us knew then to what extent the events of that day would wound him. The woods, the fields, the cry of suffering are all triggers for bringing back the horrible events of the war and will re-traumatize him for years to come.

Several years later, though, because he is a polite man and a devoted grandfather, he does return to the woods on a request from my husband Greg to go with him and our son Matt to hunt for birds. Matt's around twelve at the time and Greg bought him a gun just a short time previous to this day. The trio drives to Uncle Mac's farm, intent on spending a few hours walking through some of the wooded areas that border the now harvested potato fields. It's mid-October. The air is crisp, the trees wear their brilliant colors, and the three hunters walk single file into the woods. Dad's in the lead; Matt's the last in line. Greg remembers the feeling that came over him as they walked along. "To think that here I am out in the Maine woods, following a man who earned the Medal of Honor in World War II!" He wonders if this sortie into the woods brings back memories for his father-in-law.

Greg turns his head to see how Matt's doing, only to find that Matt isn't following behind. "Matt? Matt? Where are you? Ed, we've lost Matt!"

"Don't worry. We'll find him. You look over on the left. I'll take the right. He can't be too far from us."

After a long ten minutes of calling out and looking throughout the area, they find Matt, a bit confused about how he became lost but unharmed. Greg breathes a deep sigh of relief, Dad chuckles, and Matt sheepishly hangs his head. Dad says, "Come on, Matt. Fall in behind me. And keep that gun pointed to the ground." Grampa's now in charge of this mission, with Matt sandwiched safely between his dad and his grandfather.

The three return home without any birds but with a memorable afternoon spent together. It doesn't get better than that.

Even when the four of Dad's children become regular church attendees, accompanied by Mom for Sunday Mass, Dad remains uninvolved in the Catholic Church. Raised a Lutheran, he's a man who practices his own brand of Christian goodness without the benefit of church attendance. This practice will change when we start leaving home and Dad starts to look for meaning in his life. In the early seventies, he announces that he wants to take instruction to become a Catholic. Turning to God for help with the questions of his survival, he becomes a devout Catholic. Not content with simply going to Mass, he takes several months of instruction in the faith. Sister Mary, a kind nun who gives him individualized instruction, calls him her "best student." He wants to know the fundamental tenets of the Church, and he wants to freely discuss his questions with someone who can point him to possible answers. He finds that person in Sister Mary.

He tells Sister Mary, "I killed a lot of people in the war and I have had to live with these memories for all of these years. I question the rightness of what I did and have a hard time living with myself."

She gently reassures him, "Eddie. You were a soldier during wartime and you had no other choice. It was kill or be killed. God wanted you to live and it's your duty to discover why. Please know that you need no forgiveness. Shall we say the Lord's Prayer together?"

"Yes, and thank you, Sister."

Not long after this conversation, he receives First Communion and is later confirmed as a full member of the Catholic community. He attends Mass every Sunday, and when one of the church leaders asks him if he would

consider serving as a member of the Parish Council, he
quickly replies, "I would be honored."

When I am home from college, I attend Mass with him.
I'm struck by his devout commitment, and enjoy listening
to him sing the hymns with fervor. I hope that when he is
sitting at Mass that he finds some comfort and relief from
the memories that still trouble him these many years after
the war. Surely God will see fit to excuse this faithful
servant's 'trespasses' and to welcome his generous gifts of
time and devotion to the little church in Mars Hill, Maine.

In the early seventies I'm home from college for
Christmas vacation when Dad asks if I'd like to go with
him for the afternoon. He has food baskets from the
church to deliver to several families in the area. Never one
to pass up an opportunity to go for a ride with my father, I
eagerly don coat, boots, and mittens. It's a dry, cold day,
one that foretells of a coming snowstorm, another few
inches or a half foot to add to the already high snow banks
along the roads. It isn't snowing yet, but even if it had
been, Dad would still have gone out to deliver those
baskets. He knows about snow and about driving in it and
he knows about responsibility. He has baskets to deliver.

We stop at St. Joseph's Catholic Church in Mars Hill to
pick up the baskets, or more accurately, the cardboard
boxes full of food for Christmas dinners. Each box holds a
frozen turkey, cans of vegetables, bread, a bag of Aroostook
County potatoes, and a pumpkin pie. We load the boxes
into the backseat of the Chevrolet and start out.

The first stop is just off Route 1 in Westfield. I have
passed this house countless times on my way to Presque
Isle. It's set very close to the road and is unmistakable in
its forlornness. A two-story house in need of paint, it's
shrink-wrapped with plastic on the bottom level, an
attempt to keep the winter cold from entering. Dad drives
cautiously into the short drive which hasn't been cleared
from yesterday's snow. "I hope we don't get stuck in this.
Shouldn't be a problem. Got good snow tires on." He stops
the car but doesn't shut off the engine. "Susie, you stay

here and keep warm. It's awfully cold out. I'll just be a minute."

He picks up a box from the backseat and heads to the door. Just as he's about to drop the box in order to knock on the door, the door swings open and a smiling woman looks at him and at the box.

"What do we have here?"

"Oh, hello, Mrs. S. We've met at church. I'm Eddie Dahlgren, and this is just a little something from the church. Hope it helps you with Christmas dinner."

"Isn't that thoughtful. We certainly will put this food to good use, although I'm sure there are other parish families who need this more than we do."

"How have you been so far this winter?"

"Can't complain."

"Well, Merry Christmas."

"And, to you, too. And be sure to thank everyone at church for this basket."

Dad walks back to the car and climbs in. "Awfully nice people. They don't have a dime but they never ask for anything. You feel good about helping people like that." I think to myself that Dad is one of those "awfully nice people who never asks for anything" and I remember a generous farmer named Harry Bass who's gifted him with holiday baskets during the years when money was scarce in our household. Dad skillfully backs the car back out onto Route 1. As we continue our gifting, I continue with my silent musing about Harry Bass and earlier years when I spent time riding in the car with Dad...

Growing up, there are days during school vacations when I'd go along with Dad on his route, content to sit in the warm car, listen to the radio, and just be with Dad. Sometimes these together times would be prompted by the sparring that goes on between my mother and me. She'd have had just enough of my independent streak and would call for a break. "Why don't you go with your father for the morning?" she'd suggest, exasperated. I'd jump at the chance for the freedom of the open road.

"Volare" or "Catch a Falling Star" or some other late fifties song is playing on the radio. Dad cracks his window just a bit to let out the smoke from his constant Camel cigarette. I sing along, or just sit quietly observing the farms that we pass. If it's winter like today, Dad is likely delivering tags to farmers at their potato storage houses, tags that will be attached to the bags of potatoes, certifying them as seed for next year's crop.

Pulling off the main road to the plowed roads leading up to the potato houses, Dad leaves the car running to keep me warm. Dressed in his signature tan khakis, topped with a wool jacket and a cap tipped jauntily just a bit to the side, Dad shoots me his crooked grin as he trudges off, telling me he won't be gone long. I continue to listen to the radio, or pick out just the right shade from my box of Crayola crayons for a coloring book picture I'm working on, or pick up the pair of scissors I've brought along and cut out paper doll clothes from the other book I have with me. Before I finish with one or another of my amusements, Dad's back and we're on our way to his next stop.

When he visits Harry Bass, he parks the car on Houlton's main street rather than in front of one of Mr. Bass's potato houses. Harry Bass has an office on the second floor of a building just down the street from the cinema. Again as Dad exits the car, he assures me he won't be long. Now that we're parked in a place where I can do some people watching, I amuse myself by speculating about the lives of the people walking by, bundled up against the cold. Dad might be gone fifteen minutes or forty-five minutes. Regardless of the amount of time, I am perfectly content, away from Mom's demands.

On some of these visits, Dad reappears with Harry Bass and they cross the street to the A & P store to return just a few minutes later with a cardboard box filled with groceries. Dad opens the rear door and gently sets the box on the seat.

"Harry. This is awfully nice of you. You're too generous."

Harry smiles and says, "Eddie. I want you and your family to enjoy this and have a good holiday. Consider it a thank you for all that you've done. From me and my people." Hannukah, not Christmas, is Mr. Bass's winter holiday, but that matters not when it comes to giving holiday gifts. Although Dad never reveals much about his experience in Europe during World War II, Mr. Bass knows from newspaper accounts that Dad has fought in many bloody battles. He also knows that if it weren't for veterans like Dad, Harry's 'people' would have continued to be consumed by fire and starvation.

Over the years, Mr. Bass continues to gift our family with holiday baskets. Even after Dad retires, Harry and his driver turn into our driveway with a box full of Christmas turkey and all the fixings. And, because he is Jewish, Harry often includes a bottle of Manishevitz wine. Dad never has the heart to tell him that a rabid teetotaler rules our house and that the wine will end up down the kitchen drain...

My musings complete, I come back to the present and turn my attention to Dad who's turning into the next stop on his delivery run. Once again, we pull up to a home that has seen better times, that houses a young family who also never ask for charity. Once again, Dad steps out with the Christmas box, heading for the front door.

"Hello, Mrs. G. I'm Eddie Dahlgren from St. Joseph's Church. How are you today? How are your boys?"

"Hi, Mr. Dahlgren. I've seen you at church. Can't complain. The boys are growing like weeds and eating me out of house and home."

Dad chuckles. "I've got something here from the church that might help you with their appetites. Where would you like me to put this?"

"My goodness! How thoughtful. Here, let me show you to the kitchen table. You can put it there, Eddie. Be sure to thank everyone for this gift."

He returns to the car and repeats his now familiar mantra. "Awfully nice family. Down on their luck. You feel good doing a little bit to help them have a good meal for Christmas."

Finished with gifting for the day, we head for home, listening to holiday classics on the radio. As the words for "White Christmas" come through the radio, I am as content as anyone could possibly be, sharing an afternoon with my dad, learning much more about the essentials than I have learned at college. Although college broadens and deepens my understanding of many academic disciplines, it is always Dad who teaches me the essentials of life and reminds me of what matters in the world. Giving to others is important. Even if you have little to give in a material sense, you can give of yourself and this is what Dad has been doing ever since he returned from Europe with a chest full of medals and a heart full of sorrow for the fallen comrades with whom he served. Even when he's dog tired from walking the potato fields all day, he'll change out of his work clothes, don a dress shirt and tie and head off to a meeting of the school board. Or he'll attend an American Legion meeting, knowing that one of the fellows needs some help with the paperwork that might earn him a disability check. Or he'll skip lunch, load up the lawn mower in the trunk of the Chevrolet, and head over to the baseball field that needed mowing for the boys' game that evening. Over the years, he's created a life that matters so that he can sleep at night and have some respite from the horrible dreams of combat. And, over the years, he's been teaching his children by example that it is always better to give than to receive. And that differences in faith or background matter not; we all belong to the human race and all have the same needs for kindness and community.

Although the backseat of the Chevrolet is now empty of gift baskets, an enduring gift from my Dad resides within my core: the gift of his time, his affection and his goodness, which will be with me all the years of my life.

As we near our home on Route 1 in Blaine, the snow starts to spit and the light of day starts to wane. Still warm in the cocoon of the Chevrolet and happy to have spent a day with Dad, I look forward to the evening meal that is soon to come. It's Saturday so Mom's homemade supper will grace our table: baked beans, scalloped potatoes, cinnamon rolls, and apple pie.

Dad slows and puts on his signal to turn left into our driveway. "Looks like we finished just in time. I think we're in for a storm tonight. Good night to stay in and a maybe play a game of hearts with your brothers."

He parks the car in the garage, a new and welcome addition to our little home. He comes around behind the car and pulls on the garage door, tucking us in for the night. We open the door to the kitchen, and there are all of the familiar smells of home inviting us in from the cold. Cinnamon and nutmeg and molasses all mingle in the air as Mom greets us: "Welcome home, you two. How did your day go?"

Yes, welcome home. The sweetest words in the English language.

The values that our parents pass on to us are with us still, values that we learned at the oak kitchen table and from crawling along our sections of the potato fields during the fall harvest. As each of us graduate from high school, we leave for college, eventually marry and start our own families. We are, however, never far from our parents, both physically and in our hearts.

Although Dad never realizes his dream of using the G.I. Bill to become a civil engineer, he makes sure that each of us will have college educations. Seeing us college-educated is such a dream for him that the only time growing up I ever saw him get so mad as to threaten to take a punch at any one of us was when Mike announced that he doesn't think he'd be returning to UMaine in the fall of 1971.

"You're not going to quit school and that's that," Dad responds vehemently to Mike's announcement.

"Why? You didn't go to college and you've done okay."

"No. You're not quitting."

Back and forth they argue and Mike eventually storms out, only to return shortly with a different perspective. As Dad wishes, Mike returns to school in the fall and finishes his degree, a degree that will help him gain employment with the Immigration Service. Like his father before him, Mike is to have just one job. He retired recently after thirty-plus years working on the border between Maine and Canada.

To this day I marvel at how Dad and Mom managed to send four children to college, living as they did, paycheck to paycheck. It helped that we were all good students and received some scholarship money. And, thankfully we grew up in a time when student loans were easy to obtain. Paying back the money that allowed us each to attend college taught us not only the value of an education but also the importance of being as thrifty as possible since it did sometimes hurt each month to send off a loan payment check when we were just starting careers.

Time puts everything in perspective. I recall the many times I would return home from college during breaks and summer vacation only to leave with a fresh twenty dollar bill in my pocket, a bill that Dad would take from his wallet. At that time, when he was making under a hundred dollars a week, twenty dollars was twenty percent of his weekly pay! I am so thankful for the generosity and sacrifices of my parents.

Speaking of college, we each left home in the order in which we arrived in this world. In 1967 I started my freshman year at Boston University only to find the school much too impersonal. I transferred to UMaine-Orono and eventually earned three degrees from there. Brian left home in 1970 to attend Tufts University, majoring in Chemistry. At the end of four years, he enrolled in Tufts Dental College and joined the Navy. Upon graduation from Tufts Dental, he began a four-year commitment as a Navy dentist.

Mike followed me to UMaine, majoring in Political Science. Like his father before him, Mike spent a season or two working in potato houses after his college graduation and before landing a job with the U.S. Immigration Service.

My sister Judy stays at home while she attends Northern Maine Community College. After finishing her degree, she finds work at a printing company in Presque Isle where her excellent word processing skills become invaluable. Like her sister before her, work is also the place where she meets her future husband.

Throughout these college years, we all return home during semester breaks and for the summer. When we're lucky, we find employment to help with college expenses. And we settle back into the familiar routines of our childhoods...as if we'd never left.

Years pass and we each marry and have children. A new chapter is beginning in each of our lives and in the lives of our parents.

.....

Dad is "Grampa" to some of his grandchildren and "Bubby" to others. He isn't the kind of grandfather who gets down on the floor and helps his grandchildren build a Lincoln Log house. On the other hand, if a grandchild would like to play a game of Yahtzee or Parcheesi or a hand of gin rummy, he is part of the game, sitting at the kitchen table intent on winning. He is also not the kind of grandfather who will let you win just because you're his grandchild. Life doesn't work that way. He wants you to experience competition, friendly competition right from the start.

He's to have seven grandchildren, beginning with my son Matt and ending with the birth of Mike's son Thomas thirteen years later. His manner of grandfathering comes from his core: he's simply himself. And it works. His grandchildren love to visit and do so often. During the summer months, various grandchildren spend a week at a time visiting Nana and Grampa, getting full, both on unconditional love and on Nana's cooking.

My Matt is born November 8, 1974. We name him Matthew, meaning "a gift from God" and that he is. His full name is Matthew Edward Dahlgren Daigneault because there can be no other middle name that suits. When Matt is born, Greg and I live in Presque Isle, just fifteen miles north of my parents' house and we frequently visit them. I remember bringing Matt in from the car in his infant seat when he is just a few weeks old, plopping him and his seat down on my parent's kitchen table, and watching my parents interact with him. Matt's blue eyes meet his Grampa's and smiles break out on both faces. Matt's smile could have been gas at that age, but I like to think that he is recognizing his Grampa and acknowledging a bond that will last for over thirty years.

Greg and I move to Bangor when Matt turns one, yet the visits north still continue. During summer months, Matt and I spend a week in the County and when he's old enough to be left without me, he stays on with his grandparents and I return to Bangor. On one such return, I drive into the driveway to see Matt seated on the picnic table between Nana and Grampa, licking the biggest all-

day lollipop ever made! He waves to me but doesn't budge
from his special seat between his beloved grandparents.

I step out of the car and walk over to the picnic table.
"Oh, he was such a good boy," my mother says. "We had a
nice week. Show your mom your new shoes." In between
licks on the lollipop, Matt lifts a foot to show off his new
sneakers. From the time he starts to walk, my parents
purchase his shoes, a tradition that they will keep up until
he graduates from high school.

If grandchildren or adult children are visiting our
parents during the summer months, we always leave for
our homes with a bag or two of fresh vegetables from their
enormous garden behind the house. I remember as we
grew older, the garden grew larger and seemingly more
bountiful. Peas, green beans, carrots, cucumbers, onions,
and corn all grew in this garden, along with green tomatoes
that we'd pick and place in a brown paper bag and store in
a closet to ripen. We always left our parents with more
than we came with. Because the garden was such a part
of our parents' lives, I worried secretly when Dad
announced sometime in his 80's that he guessed he
wouldn't plant a garden. I worried that Dad's time to leave
us might be approaching. The plot eventually grew in with
grass and weeds, and today is unrecognizable as the
garden it once was.

My Matt developed his own tradition around leaving his
grandparents' house after a summer visit. As I packed a
paper bag with fresh cucumbers, corn on the cob,
potatoes, and whatever else was in season, Mom would
always offer several jars of her pickles. Matt had his own
bag and loaded it with items from Nana's cupboards, items
he just couldn't live without. "Mom, we'll need to hide these
from Dad," he says as he puts a box of Ring-Dings in the
bag. Reese's candy bars, a can of Spaghettios, Nana's
chocolate chip cookies, all find their way into the bag. We
always leave with more than we came with .... in many
ways—not only the produce and the treats go home with us
but also the love and caring that can only come from home.
We load the car. Dad always brings out my suitcase. I
buckle Matt into his car seat. Hugs, kisses, and "Come
back again soon!" and admonitions to drive safely go with

us. My parents stand in the driveway and watch us back out. As I turn onto Route 1, I look over my shoulder to give a final wave and see their return wave. How I miss that.

As the years go on, more and more grandchildren arrive, no one more beloved than any other in Dad's eyes. He is fairness personified when it comes to doling out love and affection. As it was with all of us, he attends their big events: graduations and weddings. He takes those who like golf out on the links with him. He watches them play basketball and baseball and football when he can.

And sometimes he stretches the truth just a bit with them. If Nana catches him, she gives him a solid verbal thrashing. For example, when Mike's son, Thomas, is young, his grandfather tells him that he shouldn't take too many baths because that will make him weak. This is at a time when Thomas is looking for any excuse to avoid a bath and Nana, after a week of having Thomas visit without a single bath, is trying hard to get him to clean up. Now Thomas has ammunition to throw back at his Nana's pleas. If Grampa tells him that he should avoid the water, then it must be true. Grampa, of course, is teasing him and indirectly teasing our mother. But Thomas believes and Grampa never tells him otherwise!

When he retires and is having a difficult time finding enough things to do to fill his days, Judy's daughters, Heather and Amanda, help by providing daily company. He often picks them up from school and they'll spend the afternoons with their grandparents until their parents return from work. Often they have supper with my parents, giving my mom an excuse to continue cooking hearty meals. Just as with us when we were living at home, my parents listen to the girls' accounts of their days at school and give praise for their high marks on papers that they bring for their grandparents to see. The girls have their own name for their grandfather: he's Bubby to them.

Whether he answers to Bubby or Grampa or Grandfather, he's an important part of his grandchildren's lives and they never grow too old to spend time with him, time that they come to treasure.

Family picnic at Long Lake in Aroostook County, summer of 1957. Michael is standing in the front, Brian is beside Dad who holds baby sister Judy.

BRIAN, SUSAN, LT. DAHLGREN, MICHAEL MRS. DAHLGREN, JUDITH
Hero's Family At Blaine, Me. With Honor Medal And Roll Of Winners

Dahlgren family at home in 1959, posed for Boston newspaper story.

Dad with Brian and Mike in June of 1963, prior to visit to Loring Air Force Base for Armed Services Day.

Dad on the reviewing stand with S.A.C. Commander and staff, honored guest for Armed Services Day, June 1963.

HISTORICAL MOMENT — A scene like this was repeated Monday morn-
on several eastern Maine Mountain tops as Pine Tree State citizens arose
ore dawn to honor the admittance of Hawaii as this country's 50th state.
vard Dahlgren, holder of the Congressional Medal of Honor, hoists a new
star flag over Mars Hill Mountain. Maine claimed the honor of being first
raise the new flag. (NEWS photo by Voscar)

*Dad raising the flag on Mars Hill Mountain to honor Hawaii's
statehood.*

Chapter Six

His Life's Work & The Loss of Potential

When "the great mass of GIs finally reached home after the war, they discovered that jobs, especially good jobs, were in short supply. Despite government programs to ease the transition to civilian life, especially the much-heralded G.I. Bill, unemployment among veterans was rampant—triple that of civilians in 1947" (Childers, 2009, 7).

> *"I've worked with a lot of people in my life. When you can work in an area as long as I have and you can look anybody in the eye and say I haven't cheated you, I never did anything intentionally to harm you, then I can go to bed at night as far as anything I've done in my work and I can go to sleep. At least I've got that much to say. Not as a Medal of Honor recipient, but as a man." (Edward Dahlgren, Yankee Magazine, 1981, 206).*

One of the more insidious ways that Posttraumatic Stress Disorder impacts its victims' lives is by influencing their sense of future, a future that is perceived as foreshortened. Sufferers often do not "expect to have a career, marriage, children, or a normal life span." (Reid & Wise, 1995, 191). Because of this aspect of PTSD, many sufferers never reach their true potential, settling for whatever job comes along, not pursuing advancement opportunities or education/training that might lead to more lucrative and fulfilling work.

This sense of a foreshortened future was an aspect of his PTSD that had lifelong implications for Dad and our family. Given that he never expected to come home from Europe alive, coupled with the loss of his mother and a home to come home to, Dad was simply overwhelmed with life stresses when he did return from the war. Although many soldiers would take advantage of the G.I. Bill and earn college degrees, Dad's physical and emotional status right after the war impeded his pursuit of this dream. If not for PTSD, our Dad might have become a very successful engineer. If not for PTSD, he might have earned more and not have worried so much about how he was going to provide for a growing family. If not for PTSD, he might have packed all of us in the car and headed for Texas where his buddies promised good jobs and unlimited opportunities.

Dad was very intelligent. I always marveled at how quick he was with math calculations, how easily he memorized baseball statistics, how others looked to him for solutions to problems in the community. He was highly respected and I often heard people in the community comment that he should run for public office. Despite his lack of formal education, we would always claim that our dad was the smartest man we ever knew. Late in his life, he was able to verbalize how much he regretted not having been able to go on to college. He once told one of his doctors that he would much rather have his degree than the Medal of Honor any day.

That he never expected to live out a normal life span was painfully apparent to all of us, especially on the occasion of his birthday. His health issues and PTSD lead him to believe year after year that with each passing birthday, he would not be alive for the next one. He vocalized this belief by saying, "I guess this will be my last birthday. I won't be around this time next year." We'd kid him, saying that we'd guess he'd be with us for many more years, and he'd flash us his lopsided grin, and we'd worry about the possible truth in his statement.

After returning from the war, having been in charge of his men's safety, he vowed he would never again want such a heavy responsibility. He could never accept a supervisory job where he would be in charge of evaluating employees and ultimately having to make decisions about their job security. Late in his career as a potato inspector, an opportunity for advancement to a regional supervisory position came his way, but he turned it down.

Over the years, our mother would spend considerable time thinking up strategies to get Dad to consider different work. Her concerns with his job as a potato inspector were many. She knew he worked long hours in all kinds of weather and that the work was very physical. He walked miles and miles each day and she worried that as he aged, he wouldn't be able to do this. She felt that he had more abilities than the job demanded and that he could earn more money in a job where he could use his mind. Despite her attempts, Dad dug in. She did, however, convince him to take the examination for a job as post master in Mars Hill. He took the test for her, scored highly, and with his veteran's points seemed to be a top candidate. However, he didn't live in the town that had the opening and the position went to someone else.

Before he joined the Army, Eddie Dahlgren had a good job as a machinist in Worcester, a job that was part of the war effort. When he comes home from the war, that job and many others like it are no longer available. Instead of trying his luck back in Worcester, he comes home to Maine, where the agriculture industry is usually in need of workers. Suffering from the after effects of the war, he doesn't have the capacity to look beyond what is familiar and immediate. Working in a potato house, shoveling potatoes into bags, lifting heavy bags on trucks, sweeping up after a long day of physical labor, he is simply glad to have a job. He reads the newspapers and listens to the radio and knows that many other veterans around the country aren't as lucky as he is. He is earning a paycheck, has a place to live, and is safe.

Once he secures the position as a potato inspector for the State of Maine, he's done with job hunting. Although he works long hours and walks miles every day, he is his own boss and the familiar routine is a comfort. Many weeks he puts in sixty hours on the job and never complains. Instead, he's thankful for the work which allows him to provide for his family and he enjoys his contact with the farmers whose fields he inspects. He gains a reputation as a hardworking, friendly fellow who is easy to be with.

As I've mentioned, the farmers and others in his new community never hear him talk about his experiences during the war. They gather that he's a veteran as are most men his age. Knowing this, they wonder about his take on General Eisenhower as a future president. Eisenhower has his vote. "I expect he'll be a really good leader. Cool in the face of conflict. I actually have an invitation to the inauguration. We really can't afford to go, but it's quite something to be invited." This casual exchange leads to a group of farmers secretly collecting enough money to send Dad and Mom to Washington. He packs his robin's egg blue wedding suit, along with the Medal of Honor on its blue ribbon. Ken and Ruth, Mom's cousins, offer to drive them, and they are off to D.C.

As the years go on, Dad's reputation with the farmers continues to grow. He's friendly, fair and reliable. Many times when he enters the fields of potatoes, farmers on their tractors stop what they're doing, jump off the tractor, and walk over many rows of potatoes for a short visit with him. These conversations are welcome breaks during his long days, spent mostly with just his own company, walking the miles and miles through the potato fields.

His daily routine varies with the seasons. When potatoes are in the fields, so is he. When the harvest is done and winter comes, he visits the farmers in the potato storage houses, looking for diseases that might make the potatoes not certifiable as seed for next year's crop. When farmers are ready to ship their potatoes out, Dad delivers tags that must be placed on the bags, certifying that the potatoes have been 'passed' as seed potatoes.

Brian gets lucky one summer and works alongside Dad. It's the summer of '72. Brian has just finished a year of college and is home for the summer. The previous summer, he worked at the Maine Agricultural Farm in Presque Isle where he gained some solid knowledge of potato varieties and diseases which make him an asset to Dad. For two months, they work as a team, out in the fields by 7:30 and home again at 4:30. As always, if they are working close to home, they come home for lunch.

Dad has his route and routine and instructs Brian on what he's to do. They arrive at one of the farms, park the Chevrolet, and if the day is especially warm, take a big slug of water from the water jug before starting out. "Okay, Brian," Dad points with his right index finger, wagging it in his own distinctive way, "you start over here and I'll take this next section." Dad measures out the field in a grid and with that index finger, shows Brian the grid.

As they walk the rows, they keep count of what they see: the number of different varieties of potatoes, the number of various diseases. Dad's job, as I've said, is to certify a farmer's potatoes as being pure enough and healthy enough to be used as seed for the next season. Each field is allowed a certain percentage of mixture but some diseases mean that not only the field but the entire crop has to be "turned down," meaning that the potatoes cannot be used as seed but have to be sold as "table stock," potatoes that are okay to eat but not to plant.

Leaf roll and mosaic are two fungal diseases they watch for. Later in the season, they look for blight or the dreaded ring rot which instantly disqualifies a crop from being used as seed. There are many popular varieties of potatoes planted in Aroostook at that time and inspectors need to be able to distinguish one from the other. There are Kathadins, Kennebecs, Russets, Green Mountains, and Cobblers.

During some of their pass-throughs, Brian and Dad see farmers on their tractors, watering their fields or they'll stop by their houses to tell the farmers what they've found. "Crop looks good, Brad. Should be a good yield. Let's hope for a bit of rain, though." "You're right, Eddie. We sure could use some rain."

Those are pleasant conversations when all is well in the fields. On the other hand, if there's bad news, then there's tension. Money and reputation are at stake: seed potatoes are sold for more money, and a farmer's reputation as a grower of seed potatoes is worth much in the county. One season, Dad has to give our Uncle Mac bad news.

Uncle Mac is extended family and at our house frequently for Sunday suppers and always for holiday meals. A confirmed bachelor, he enjoys the chance to get a home-cooked meal and maybe play a hand of cards with his brother-in-law and nephews. Mac and his brothers raise about 150 acres of potatoes, enough in the sixties and seventies to support three families. He's known as a good farmer and a smart businessman. He is also known for his short Irish temper!

Dad has inspected Mac's fields for years and every year, the crop is excellent. But late in one growing season in the mid-1970s, Dad finds ring rot in one of the fields. When an inspector finds this particular disease, he has to carefully dig the whole plant from the field, complete with the growing tubers, sack it and show the farmer while telling him the verdict.

Dad walks up to the potato house where Mac is working. He's not looking forward to this conversation. "Hi, Mac."

"Ed. How you doing? Have you been down to look at the fields? Great looking crop this year, right?" Mac is all smiles with a mouth full of chewed up cigar. He spits a wad of loose tobacco on the floor of the potato house.

"Good crop, you're right. But I found something today I want to show you." Dad opens up the sack and points out the infected parts of the plant.

"It's ring rot, isn't it?" Mac says. He lets loose with a torrent of expletives, blaming everyone in the area for selling him bad seed, blaming among other things his neighbor for the wind that blows bad spores over to his fields. His face is beet red, his eyes behind the coke-bottle-bottom glasses he wears wide open and gleaming. "Ed. I'm not upset with you. You know that. You're just doing your job. But..." And off he goes on another round of never-before-heard expletives. He kicks a tire or two on the tractor just for good measure. Huffing and puffing, he's finally done.

"I'm awfully sorry to have to tell you that I can't certify your crop."

"I know. I know. It's not your fault. Well, what can you do?"

"My guess is that you could swallow a few glasses of Jack Daniels around supper time to ease the pain but other than that, it is as it is."

The two talk for a while longer, and then it's time for Dad to get to the next farm.

"Ed, just tell me. What about that damn Smith's potatoes? Any rot in his?"

Dad laughs, knowing about the rivalry between these two. "Haven't found anything yet."

"Damn."

My siblings and I are to know the potato harvest intimately once we are old enough to get up at the crack of dawn and crawl hour after long hour through the rows of dug potatoes, picking them up in wooden baskets made by the Native American people in neighboring New Brunswick, and dumping the baskets in large wooden barrels which we then tag, an action that results in a pay envelope on Saturday afternoons. A decided highlight to our days in the fields is spotting our dad, walking down the field, looking the crop over. He has many farms and many fields to visit during the season, and we never know when he might show up in one of our fields. But when he does, it's a proud moment. There he is, dressed in his signature suntans with a weathered baseball cap on his head, the brim pulled just the right angle to the side of his face, walking toward us. Sometimes he'll hop on the tractor beside Uncle Mac and talk for a bit as Mac finishes up a row. Other times, he'll chat with the truck drivers waiting with their crews to hoist the filled barrels of potatoes onto the flatbeds of their trucks.

Always during his visit, he'll walk down the row, greeting each of the workers, asking how things are going. I might be sitting on a full barrel of potatoes, my section all picked, and he'll stop by. He looks over at Mike, crawling along, many rows behind, picking the potatoes off the ground one at a time with only one hand, the other hand and arm draped across his basket.

"Not the swiftest picker I've seen," Dad says and we both chuckle.

"I'll probably have to help him finish up before the day ends."

"Either that or he'll miss his supper." And then he'll move on, greeting everyone until he's at the end of the row. I watch him hop on the running board of a fully-loaded flatbed, heading for the potato house, hitching a ride back to his car. Like our days, his are long and continue until he's made all of the stops on his list, arriving home at the end of the day just in time for supper.

I remember those days as if they happened just yesterday and if I close my eyes and allow stillness to enter, I can still see Dad, walking those potato rows, stopping to talk with the picking crew and Uncle Mac and I am filled with a longing that won't go away. Oh, for those days again.

For Dad as for us, the potato fields of Aroostook County defined us. Although our harvest days ended with college, Dad would continue to work until health issues forced an early retirement when he was 62. After he retired, restless for work, he was sometimes fortunate to obtain work with farmers who needed their potatoes 'rogued'. Roguing involves pulling up 'volunteers', potatoes that are not the dominant variety, and other plants that look blighted or somehow unhealthy. Farmers who are trying to get contracts with major companies will pay to have their fields 'rogued' so as to help their chances of landing those contracts. That farmers called Dad was evidence of their respect for his knowledge. One of the area farmers was trying to get a contract with Frito Lay which was known to be very, very fussy. When they successfully landed the contract, the Frito Lay representative told them that the man they hired to 'rogue' their potatoes was the best he'd seen at it. That comment got back to Dad who felt very good at having been recognized for doing a good job.

Picture of Dad in his 'suntans' in 1950.

Chapter Seven

PTSD Returns in Force: The Difficult Decades 1980's and 1990's

"A longitudinal study of WWII veterans reports that heavy combat exposure was associated with increased likelihood of death or chronic illness before age 65" (Schnurr & Spiro, 1999, 353).

"The combat veteran who has experienced substantial trauma attempts to avoid thinking about the experience or sharing war experiences with others. This avoidance is associated with physiological work. Over time, such inhibition places cumulative stress on the body, which increases the likelihood of stress-related disease (cardiovascular syndromes, ulcerative colitis, joint pain) (Elder, Shanahan & Clipp, 1997, 335).

"In this study, the authors examined the effect of retirement on psychological and physical symptoms in 404 older male veterans. As expected, the PTSD group experienced greater increases in psychological and physical symptoms during retirement, relative to the other group." (Schnurr, Lunney, Sengupta & Spiro, 2005, 561).

Soldiers who physically survive their war experiences to return home, return changed at the deepest levels of their beings. Having been faced with performing unimaginable and never ending slaughter of an enemy, our soldiers question their goodness, their very pre-war identities, and wonder who they are now and how they will live now.

"Socrates taught that the soul is that which distinguishes good from evil. What are the consequences to the soul, then, if we must kill or destroy? Or if we do not believe in the cause for which we are fighting?" (Tick, 2005, 110).

"Concern with morality is pervasive among soldiers and veterans, is often uppermost in their minds, and can remain with them until death" (112).

When the pain of angina first begins, Dad shrugs it off, expecting it to pass, thinking this new pain is likely from a pulled muscle in his chest. He's most probably lifted something too heavy, not realizing that he's getting older and can't do everything that he used to do when he was younger. But the pain doesn't pass—it grows worse. The first of these "worsts" occurs on a memorable day.

We are all in Boston, gathered to celebrate Brian's graduation from Tufts Dental School and initiation as a Naval officer. It's a windy afternoon as we hurry towards the John Hancock Building for the ceremony. Our family party includes Mom, Dad, Judy, Matthew and me. It is spring 1976, and Matt is two at the time, dressed to the nines in a tan suit I made him for the occasion. His little legs are having trouble keeping up so his Grampa scoops him up and carries him in his strong arms. I won't know until weeks later that Dad was in tremendous pain at the time, angina pain that felt like his heart was being squeezed in a vice.

A few weeks after returning home from Brian's graduation, the pain worsens and Dad decides he needs to see his doctor, who immediately hospitalizes him for tests and observation. While awaiting an official diagnosis of angina and the requisite prescription for nitroglycerin, his doctor gives him a warning. "Ed, it's time to give up smoking...if you want to live for a few more years."

With the same steely willpower we've observed in Dad for years, he quits "cold turkey" a habit that's been a part of his life for over forty years. A two-pack-a-day guy, he quits with nothing but his own brand of personal resolve. The withdrawal from nicotine is sheer hell, but he sees it through. From the day he determines to quit until the day he leaves us, he never smokes another cigarette.

He quits smoking but the pain from the angina and kidney stones finally force him to take an early retirement from his long workdays walking the potato fields of Aroostook County. He has worked as a potato inspector for over thirty years. At 62, he finds himself with a lot of time on his hands and hours of emptiness to fill.

When he gives his retirement notice to his area supervisor and the main office in Augusta, he not only loses his daily routine but also the Department of Agriculture pick-up truck he's used for the last few years. For most of his working life, he's used the family car for work so having a state vehicle was a welcome feature of his job. Given the bumpy, often muddy, field roads that he has to drive through for work, the truck is a much more practical vehicle than any of his Chevrolets ever were. He's kept the pick-up in top-notch condition, taking it to his favorite local garage for regular servicing, just like he always does for his own car.

A few days after he's given his notice, two Department of Agriculture employees drive into his driveway. Dad comes out to greet them. They tell him they've come for the pick-up. "Thanks a lot, Eddie. Good luck." And they're gone, one of them at the wheel of the pick-up.

Dad comes back into the house and says, "Well, I guess that's it." This minute-long exchange in his driveway is what passes for a retirement party, that and a letter from Augusta that arrives a few weeks later.

It isn't the lack of fanfare at his retirement that troubles Dad. He's never been one to seek the limelight. What troubles him is how to spend his days. With retirement and time on his hands, it becomes increasingly more difficult to keep PTSD in the shadows. The winter months are especially hard for him. Depression surfaces, along with anxiety, and his problems with sleep worsen. Now without the familiar routine of work, he has too much idle time to think and unbidden memories resurface, especially memories of that day on Winter Street in

Oberhoffen.   The first winter of his retirement was perhaps the worst. In order to provide some structure to his days, every day he walks the mile from our house to the post office in Mars Hill, checks on the mail, and during the winter months, continues on to the Legion hall where he starts a fire in the basement woodstove. Eventually a group of fellow retirees, some Legion members and others not, gather during the afternoons for cards. The camaraderie of these gatherings and the opportunity to practice his considerable skill at winning any kind of card game help to pass the time. At the end of an afternoon of woodstove warmth and friendly banter, he puts on his coat and hat and walks the mile back home. Most afternoons, several cars stop and familiar faces offer him a ride. He's well known and well liked, and well-meaning neighbors stop without realizing that he needs to walk, for the exercise and for the way that a walk helps fill up his time.

Dad's faith helps him to find some peace from the memories of his war but does not entirely keep his worsening depression at bay. He can't sleep. He gets up in the middle of the night, goes to the bathroom, opens the medicine cabinet door, and scans the selection of over-the-counter pain relievers and sleep-aids lined up on the shelf, looking for something with a label that says 'can make you drowsy,' for him a welcome side effect.

He takes two tablets from the container and washes them down with a short paper cup of water, then returns to bed hoping for some relief. Even when and if sleep comes, his nights are frequently disturbed by vivid and horrific flashbacks of battles that happened so many years ago.

The flashbacks make him sit up suddenly in bed, startled awake by the unrelenting booming of the big guns, followed by the crashing and crumbling of buildings and soldiers crying out, "I'm hit. Help!" Some nights it's German voices he hears coming closer as he clings to life on a mountain in Italy. Sometimes it's the unmistakable stench of intestines spilling their contents on the ground beside a dying man that startles him awake. And the rats.

The musky smelling rodents, squeaking nearby, crunching, crunching, crunching through flesh and bone. He cries out in his sleep, "Get away. Get away." The most horrific scenes are those where he is nearly face-to-face with a German soldier, close enough to recognize the other's youth and the unmistakable blue of his eyes, close enough to see the muzzle of the man's rifle trained on his midsection. Then there is the memory of his pulling the trigger of his Tommy gun, the enemy's blood splattering out from a mortal chest wound, some of it warm and wet as it hits his killer in the face, and then the thud as the man hits the ground. Night after night this parade of moving pictures marches behind his closed eyes, awake or asleep.

He speaks with one of his doctors about getting a prescription for a sleep medication. He gets the scrip filled at the local pharmacy, hoping that finally he'll be able to sleep that night. When a particular medication's potency wears thin, he returns to his doctor with a request for something "stronger" and once again, tries another remedy. Although the medication provides some relief, it also leads to dependency and to a wish for nothing more than sleep.

As his depression deepens, he withdraws from us. He becomes more and more preoccupied with only the relief that sleep might bring. He is losing his war, and we feel helpless as to how to help him. And during one of these painful periods, our mother is in the hospital with a serious heart condition. Dad's anxiety is ramped to the max.

Mom returns home from the hospital only to find Dad's condition worsening by the day. He isolates himself at home, wanting only to sleep, his once sharp mind now fogged by sleeping pills and pain medication. Mom is worried that he might be suicidal. She asks Dale, my sister Judy's husband, to take Dad's old hunting rifle for safekeeping. She calls her adult children, complaining about Dad's unresponsiveness, saying "He just needs to get out of bed and get going. There's nothing wrong with him." What she doesn't realize is that he is critically ill. Finally, one of his doctors, growing more concerned with Dad's ever more frequent complaints about pain and difficulty sleeping, realizes that it is time to recommend a different form of treatment. This doctor makes an appointment for Dad with a local psychiatrist with the hope that therapy and appropriate medication might help.

As per men of his generation, Dad goes reluctantly to his first appointment. It is 1994 when he first steps into Dr. Stuart Wyckoff's office in Presque Isle. Accompanied by Mom to his appointment, he figures he can always tell the doctor that his wife made him come to the appointment. Reluctantly at first, he keeps going to future appointments because he is finding some relief from his struggles. Medication combined with an opportunity to talk every week helps him relax and get some relief from the insomnia that plagues him. At first he meets with his therapist weekly; as the years go by, ten in total, appointments eventually are months apart. These last years of his life are likely the most comfortable for him. He is more available to us, his loving family, and seems to get some joy out of his days. Towards the end of his treatment, he mentions to me, "You know. I really don't need to talk to Dr. W. anymore, but I guess it doesn't do any harm, does it?"

"No, Dad. It doesn't do any harm. So keep going."

Dad will suffer from depression and anxiety for the rest of his life, but fortunately the two conditions respond to treatment. We know that the anxiety is just tentatively kept in check by his worry about prescription refills arriving in time via the mail from the U.S. Veterans Hospital near Augusta. Sometimes, he'll become so agitated that Mom has to call the V.A. to see where his medications are. When she doesn't feel that she has a satisfactory answer, she asks to speak to the director of the center. When she explains the reason for her call and provides the information that her husband in a Medal of Honor recipient, the director assures her that he will take care of the problem. From that point forward, Dad's medication always arrives on time.

During his talks with his therapist, Dad tells only one story about his war. He describes the day in Oberhoffen, the day which leads to his nomination for the Medal of Honor. This conversation happens around the time that the movie *Saving Private Ryan* is playing in all of the theaters. His doctor wonders if Dad will see the movie and learns at his next appointment that Dad did see the movie with our mother and two granddaughters. With both granddaughters holding his hands throughout the movie, he watches the scenes that he will later say are much like his own combat experience. When his doctor asks Dad about the experience of watching the movie, he replies, "Well, Doc, I made it through World War II. Watching that movie was nothing compared to the real thing."

So, what were the topics of all those other sessions if not about his war? When I visit his former therapist in August of 2010, wanting only to hear about the doctor's opinion of Dad's PTSD, I am told, "Your father was so proud of all of you. I probably know more about you and your siblings than you realize. I remember when you left for North Carolina and your Dad's telling me about that. Every session was an update on how each of you were doing. His children are his legacy, much more so than his Medal of Honor. He once told me, 'Doc, I'd rather have your medical degree any day than the Medal.'" Here is a poignant reference to his lack of education and his deep-seated desire for it. No wonder he was so proud of our academic accomplishments.

"I liked your dad and I think I helped him with his depression and anxiety. As far as his PTSD, I would say he suffered for fifty years with the fallout from the war. By the time I started seeing him, he must have encapsulated that experience somewhere inside and didn't want to dig it up."

For 10 years from the mid-1990's and on into the next decade, Dad will visit with Dr. Wyckoff and over time, we start to see subtle changes in our dad. Mike recalls that with Dr. Wyckoff's help, "Dad would talk a little more about things from when he was younger, not necessarily war related things but other events from growing up. He also seemed to laugh a lot more easily, was less private and could open up and be relaxed, not on edge as before."

During these ten years, he comes to look forward to his talks with his therapist, enjoys his grandchildren and grown children who visit frequently, loves playing golf in Mars Hill with other aging residents, and settles into a routine of cribbage games with friends during winter afternoons. As those friends pass on, he begins again to wonder about his own longevity. Who would have guessed it? He attends Mass every Sunday and likely leaves the question of his survival in the hands of his God.

Although his bothersome PTSD symptoms seem to be in check, other health issues continue to plague him. Kidney stones still form and the agony of getting rid of them seems to never end. His heart condition worsens, and he is hospitalized for congestive heart failure. In his eighties, he is diagnosed with diabetes and suffers from having to give up his love affair with sweets, especially our mother's homemade kind. What he suspects is arthritis in his hip forces him to sometimes use a cane. Despite these physical conditions, his mood is generally positive. We know he feels well when he gets back to his lifetime habit of teasing our mother!

As the years pass, Dad becomes a revered elder statesman of sorts, often called upon to address a group or raise the flag on national holidays. With his anxiety in check, he's more able to speak in public, and when he senses that a request to do so is his patriotic duty, he will accept the invitation. He treats these occasions with utmost respect, dressing carefully in his signature navy blue sport coat, grey dress slacks, white shirt, and striped tie. In 1995, he is asked to address a group of our country's newest patriots, a group of individuals who will become American citizens at the end of the day's ceremony. He asks my brother, Mike, if he would draft a few remarks for the day. The speech he gives that day is largely my brother's writing, with some editing by Dad. I feel strongly that Mike captures Dad's spirit in the words that Dad delivers.

The ceremony is held in Mars Hill at the high school gymnasium, a change from previous venues for these ceremonies. Invited guests include local dignitaries, families of the soon-to-be new citizens, and the excited group for whom the ceremony is organized. Introduced as the guest speaker for the occasion, Dad comes up to the podium, lays his papers in front of him, dons his glasses, and looks out over the crowd.

"Having lived in this area for 46 years and worked as a seed potato inspector for over thirty years in Mars Hill, Blaine, Bridgewater, Monticello, Littleton, and Houlton, it is a pleasure to see the number of applicants who are to be naturalized today who are from these small towns. Prior to 1991 these ceremonies were held in the courts, and in the past the speakers at the ceremonies were usually politicians. Let me be clear. I am not a politician but I hope that the remarks I am about to make will be meaningful to you.

A few months ago, a columnist for the *Bangor Daily News*, Mr. Tom Weber, wrote of his observations after attending a naturalization ceremony held in Orono, Maine. He noted, in so many words, that such an event is one of the nicest, most dignified, and most under-publicized affairs presented by our government. It is perhaps all of these descriptions because of the very personal nature of the ceremony. You who are becoming naturalized citizens are making a very, very important personal decision that will affect not only you but everyone who lives in the United States.

I think the fact that you are all here because you *want* to be here is exactly what makes today mean so much. You are not forced to be here by anyone. You who are becoming United States citizens today came to this country by choice. For your own reasons, you made the United States your home. By becoming citizens, you are taking what can be considered the most important step in the choice you made several years ago, when you first came here to live. All of us here today feel a certain sense of pride in what you are doing and you all have the right to be very proud yourselves.

Often, speakers at these ceremonies make it a point to remind you of your responsibilities as United States citizens. I think this point has been well taken in recent years, especially here in the state of Maine. The number of people eligible to vote who actually do get out and cast a ballot has grown remarkably. There is probably no single

thing you as citizens can do that is more important. By
voting, you are saying that you care what happens in this
country, and *believe* it, the men and women you elect to
public office know it.

Being a responsible citizen means more than voting,
though. It means becoming involved. You who have come
here today to become our newest Americans already know
about being involved. I can look out at you and see several
of you whom I know personally. You all have your own
story to tell. You, our newest citizens, are the folks who
work in our stores and manufacturing plants. You are the
folks that help take care of our children. You plant our
crops, tend to our sick and elderly, and serve our country
in the Armed Forces. You are teachers. You are
homemakers. You might like country music or you might
like rock and roll. You get up in the morning and go off to
work, complain a little or a lot about your taxes, worry
about making ends meet, and wonder if the Red Sox will
ever win a World Series. You are already what makes the
United States of America a symbol of hope for people all
over the world. There may be some of you here today who
are children. You are becoming citizens at what might be
the best and most important time in your lives. You are
here because your new parents care enough to adopt you
and bring you to America, to give you a new and better
chance.

We all find it upsetting and discouraging to read and
hear about crime, violence and despair here in America
and in other parts of the world. It is important for everyone
to remember that the absolute vast majority of people are
decent and honest. You cannot just throw up your hands
and give up. By making the choice you have made, to
become citizens of the United States, you are showing your
commitment to making this country and the world a better
place in which to live.

Many years ago, I was called by my country to serve in
a most terrible war. Like the other men and women who
were called to duty, I did my part and came home, to make
a living and raise a family. I can remember how it seemed
that we would never again as a country have to go to war.
Those feelings soon disappeared as we were drawn into the

Korean Conflict and the war in Vietnam. Today, we find ourselves again being looked to by other nations as strife, war and famine engulf different parts of the world. Our leaders are faced with very difficult decisions to make. You, as United States citizens, can help our leaders by speaking out, by voicing your opinions, by becoming involved in the whole process. You must let your elected officials know what you think should be done. The easy way out is to do nothing, but if you make that choice, then nothing will get done.

You must also never forget that, for all its faults, there is no other country on Earth like the United States of America. Here you have so many freedoms that can only be dreamed of in other lands. Our Founding Fathers put a document together over two hundred years ago that still stands. No other country in the world can make such a statement. Remember that this document gives the rights of freedom to you, the people. The government does not grant rights. We, the people of the United States, grant the government the authority to conduct business. If the government misuses that trusted authority, then we, the people, are responsible for seeing that such misuse ceases. You accomplish this by exercising your rights as guaranteed by our Constitution. Remember the cold, hard fact that many men and women gave their lives to ensure that you retain those basic rights. Hang on to them dearly and do not take them for granted.

In closing, I hope that each of you will hold on to the memory of this day and will not forget how important your decision to become a United States citizen really is. The certificate you receive today is far more than just a pretty piece of paper. There are literally millions of people in the world who would give everything they have for that certificate. Be proud, be caring, and give of yourselves to make our country and our world a better place in which to live. Thank you and congratulations."

In addition to medication and therapy, it is Dad's involvement in veterans' projects that help to fill his days and provide him with a level of satisfaction that his life does matter. Of all the boards and committees that Dad serves on during his many years of giving to his community and to the greater community of Aroostook County, the work that he does as a member of a steadfast band of veterans from all over the County is what gives him the most positive personal satisfaction. This group of twenty men and women drive from their homes at least one day a month for ten years to do the necessary work to obtain funding for the creation of a veteran's nursing home in Aroostook County in Northern Maine. A decade earlier, this same group of veterans had been successful, with then U.S. Senator George Mitchell's help, in getting an outpatient diagnostic care clinic established at Cary Medical Center in Caribou. The clinic was set up initially as a pilot program for veterans in rural areas, to perform routine screenings, x-ray and blood work, to determine if the veteran required hospitalization or further care at the V.A. hospital in Togus, Maine. Even before the establishment of this clinic, it was a known fact that only twenty out of every thousand veterans in Northern Maine sought health care at Togus, a round-trip of 550 miles for veterans living in the Caribou area. Given that 9,500 veterans were living in Aroostook County in the 1980s, this population was gravely underserved. If visits to the clinic exceeded veterans' visits to Togus, this would serve as evidence of not only a need for health services locally, but also evidence of a willingness on the part of veterans to access such services.

The clinic is such a huge success that strategic planning for writing a bill to establish a nursing home in Aroostook County begins almost at once. The measure sponsored by Speaker of the House John Martin (D-Eagle Lake) sweeps through both the Maine House and Senate without debate. When it lands on then Governor Joseph Brennan's desk, it earns his signature without hesitation. Official ground breaking ceremonies for the Maine Veteran's Home in Caribou, Maine, are scheduled for May 7, 1988. Among the dignitaries present for the ceremony is Dad, who gives the salute to the flag, another proud moment in his life.

He and the other members of the original group who worked so hard to make this idea a reality are named to the Aroostook County Veterans' Medical Research and Development Board of Trustees. Although a new nursing home will be built and ready in two years to serve the needs of those veterans who served their country, the trustees' work is not finished. The initial funding for the building project does not cover a proposed chapel, alcove and recreation area. In order for these features to be a part of the structure, an additional $105,000 in private funds needs to be raised. The trustees go to work, contacting veterans' organizations, businesses, civic groups, and individuals. The group is so successful that by the time of the open house for the nursing home, scheduled for Saturday, January 6, 1990, the funds have been secured and the facility includes the additional features.

The members of this first Board of Directors include Walter Corey, Clement Lynch, Edward Dahlgren, Dewey Ouellette, George Berube, Roberta Guerrette, Mary Ann Rowe, James Wark, Denis Drew, Robert Goley, Meo Bosse, George Morin, Val Jandreau, Everett Roberts, Jack Stewart, Albert Gahagan, Richard Pratt, Roy Doak, Bill Flagg, and Ray Guerrette.

"Most of us here will never have to face what he faced—because he faced it." U.S. Senator George Mitchell at the dedication ceremony of Dahlgren Hall, Loring A.F.B., July 3, 1986.

Had Dad had been less fortunate and not survived his war, Loring Air Force Base in Aroostook County might have been known by another name: Dahlgren Air Force Base. As it was, the base was named for another Medal of Honor recipient, one Charles Loring, an Air Force pilot from Portland, Maine, who died of injuries while fighting in Korea. Bases are usually named posthumously for military heroes. Given this fact, I believe our family got a better deal than the Loring family. Years after the base is established, Dad receives the following letter:

24 March 86

Dear Mr. Dahlgren:

In June of this year, we will be dedicating a brand
new dining hall at Loring. The new facility is
primarily for the use of our assigned enlisted men
and women. We have been considering what might
be an appropriate name for the new building.
We would very much like to dedicate the new dining
hall as Dahlgren Hall in memory of your courageous
acts which led to the award of the esteemed
Congressional Medal of Honor.

With your permission, we will proceed with planning
a suitable dedication ceremony time to coincide with
the opening of the new dining hall. We would be
exceedingly proud and pleased to honor you in this
way and allow the memory of your deeds to inspire
those who follow you in dedicated service to our
country.

Sincerely,

John T. Shepard, Colonel, USAF
Commander

When Dad opens the letter and reads it, he turns to
Mom. "Polly. What do you think of this? Pretty nice, huh?"
She reads the letter and concludes, "Very nice."
Dad contacts Colonel Shepard, thanks him for this
honor and assures the colonel that he and his family will
attend the dedication ceremony.

The ceremony, scheduled for July 3, 1986, features
Dad and U.S. Senator George Mitchell as speakers. I recall
vividly how Dad stands at the podium, looking every bit the
professional speaker in suit and striped tie. He has come a
long way from the time in 1945, newly back from the war,

when 1000 citizens from the Caribou area came together to honor him and he stammered uncontrollably. Today, he is in charge and looking comfortable. He begins his remarks, which he's handwritten on note paper:

"I am very pleased and honored today to have this beautiful hall called 'Dahlgren Hall.' Many times halls such as this are named in memory of someone who is no longer living, but I am pleased to know that my children and grandchildren can say, when they come to this place, that this hall is named after their father or grandfather. I'm sure the thousands of military people stationed here at Loring will enjoy this facility very much, now and in the future.

"I never dreamed when growing up and going to school in Woodland and Caribou, which are within thirty miles of here, that this would happen to me but in this country, these things are possible. I really am one of the lucky ones, to come back from combat okay. I have a fine wife, four good children, six grandchildren, and many friends, so I am very thankful. For reasons unknown, many of my friends as well as others didn't come back. They gave their lives for their country. They are the heroes.

"I would like to thank Senator Mitchell on behalf of all the veterans in Aroostook County. He has always been very cooperative and helpful anytime we contacted him. I'd also like to thank Mary LeBlanc who works in Senator Mitchell's office.

"And, I'd like to thank the people responsible for this dedication: Colonel O'Malley, Captain Kearns, Lieutenant Berkholtz, and Airman Rudy Castello. And have a good Fourth of July weekend."

Senator Mitchell speaks next. "Most of us here will never have to face what he faced because he faced it." Applause breaks out and the Senator has to stop his remarks until the crowd quiets down. The ribbon cutting comes next and is handled by Dad and Senator Mitchell, who then lead the rest of the guests into the dining hall. This will be the first of many meals that we'll eat at this facility. Told that he isn't expected ever to pay for a meal, having paid full price in France over forty years ago, Dad still always pays full price. To him that is simply the right thing to do.

As Dad ages, other honors from his state and community pile up. In 1976, he is invited to a ceremony at the Veterans Administration Center in Togus, Maine, a ceremony which commemorates the Medal of Honor and specifically honors Dad, the only MOH recipient at that time still residing in the state of Maine. During the ceremony, he plants a commemorative tree on the hospital grounds and uncovers a new plaque that describes the Medal of Honor. Today, when my husband and I visit Togus, we see the tree, large and healthy, and we remember the special day when it was planted.

In the mid-eighties, Dad is invited to the Blaine House to receive a special license plate from then governor, Joseph Brennan. Many of his family members are with him to witness this event, including my ten-year-old son Matt, who is invited to sit in the governor's chair! The license plate, which Dad holds in front of him for a newspaper photo, has in large print the abbreviation "MH1" and a picture of the Medal of Honor. Underneath these are the words, "Valor Above and Beyond the Call of Duty". From this time on, the special plate is the only one ever displayed on my parents' cars. Many times when the car is parked in a public place, people will walk over to ask him what that license plate means. Humble as ever, he gives a very brief explanation and most people walk away, awed that they have met this true Maine hero.

But it's late in his life when Dad gets the surprise of his life: he is awarded a high school diploma. The story follows...

Dad is a sharp tack and not much gets by him. A card buddy can bluff all he wants, but Dad usually wins. What we hope might be a surprise for him never is: he always finds out what's going on. On one rare occasion, though, he's duped.

June 8, 2001, Central Aroostook High School gymnasium: a packed house waits for the familiar strains of "Pomp and Circumstance" to begin, announcing the arrival of yet another graduating class. Proud parents and grandparents rise to the music, focus their cameras, waiting for a glimpse of the graduate they are here to honor. In this graduating class is my niece, Heather Johnston. Heather will be giving the valedictory address.

The students' speeches complete, Superintendent Roger Shaw takes the stage. He begins his remarks:

"'THE GREATEST GENERATION' was the term coined by veteran newsman Tom Brokaw to describe a generation of citizens whose character was shaped during this country's Great Depression, who rescued the world from the grip of Nazi oppression, and for those fortunate enough to return, built a nation of greatness on the foundation of freedom which came only through the great price they paid. Recently, on Memorial Day, we again consecrated the memories of those who made the ultimate sacrifice so we could sit here this evening, in freedom, and celebrate the accomplishments of this fine group of young people who are now on the threshold of facing the challenges of their own generation.

"Tonight we have honored members of the Class of 2001 for their achievements and will momentarily be awarding diplomas as a reward for the hard work and perseverance demonstrated by each graduate.

"I would ask Board Chairman Steve Robinson and Principal Ed Buckley to join me as we honor not a graduating senior but a community member who has consistently demonstrated the virtues of sacrifice, perseverance, hard work, civic responsibility, family devotion, and unwavering faith."

In on the secret from the beginning, Mom knows that Roger Shaw is referring to Dad. Dad, oblivious to the honor that is about to come his way, is busy watching the crowd. "Ed. Pay attention. He's talking about you!" exclaims Mom.

Dad perks up, eyes front and forward, and listens to what Roger is saying. "What do you mean? Why's he talking about me?"

"Just listen. You'll see."

"Born in the small town of Perham, Maine, he grew up in Colby Siding and attended Caribou High School. On June 12, he and his wife will celebrate their fifty-third wedding anniversary. Together they raised their four children and fostered in them high standards of social responsibility and academic excellence.

He was employed by the State of Maine for thirty-seven years as a seed potato inspector. He served on the Blaine Town Council and was a charter member of the SAD #42 Board of Directors. He is a communicant at St. Joseph's Parish in Mars Hill and a member of the Knights of Columbus.

He served as a member of the Board of Directors for the Veterans Nursing Home in Caribou for ten years and was instrumental in getting that facility built in Aroostook County. He served on the Blue Cross/Blue Shield Board of Maine and was a founding member of the Mars Hill and Blaine Recreation Association. He is a life member of the Veterans of Foreign Wars, the American Legion, the Disabled American Veterans, the Military Order of World Wars, the Military Order of Purple Hearts, and the National Order of Battlefield Commissions.

In the village of Oberhoffen, France, his character and courage were put to the ultimate test, and because of his heroic acts of fearless bravery in the face of grave danger, he was awarded the nation's highest military award, the Congressional Medal of Honor. He is one of 154 living Medal of Honor recipients in the United States, and the only one living in Maine.

His love of community and country, and the honesty, integrity, and humility which have permeated every aspect of his life, have provided us all with a resplendent example of how a life should be lived.

His greatest legacy, however, may be his lifetime love, commitment, and devotion to his wife, children, and grandchildren.

On behalf of the SAD #42 Board of Directors, would you all please join us in honoring and thanking a time-tested member of "The Greatest Generation," and a true American hero, Mr. Edward C. Dahlgren. Ed, I am proud and honored to make this presentation of an Honorary Diploma from Central Aroostook High School to you."

Dad, humble as always, rises from his seat to the resounding standing ovation that his community is giving him and makes his way to the front of the gymnasium. Reminiscent of the manner in which he shook President Truman's hand so many years ago, he reaches out to shake Mr. Shaw's hand. "Thank you. Thank you, Roger, for your kind words and for this award. I had no idea."

"You're most welcome, Ed, and most deserving of this diploma." Dad turns to face the crowd, which is still standing, and returns to his seat, perhaps the proudest graduate of the Class of 2001.

The next few years are perhaps the best years of Dad's life. More comfortable with himself since therapy, he is able to laugh more and enjoy each day. Aches and pains aside, we know he's doing well when he continues to play golf well into his 80's. Many of my happiest times with Dad are times we spend on the golf course in the shadow of Mars Hill Mountain.

Dad takes up golf late in life when an enterprising local family builds a golf course on the side of the mountain. Dad is hungry for a hobby during the long days of his retirement and I venture that his longevity can be partially attributed to his hours of exercise and socializing that come via his involvement with golf.

He takes up golf about the same time as my son is becoming a golfer himself, participating on his high school golf team and later on the University of Maine at Farmington's team. My husband Greg has always been a golfer so I decide to give the sport a try myself, thinking of all the wonderful family times to be had with my "boys" on the links. Both much better golfers than I will ever be, Matt and Greg tolerate my slow and deadly delivery, never knowing where my ball might land. Knowing that I am no match for them, on future outings I just hit a few strokes on each hole, pick up my ball if I can find it, and plop it down on the green, hoping that the little white ball will miraculously find its way into the hole in less than five attempts.

I know that playing with my little family isn't much fun for them but playing with Dad is a different story. I now have something extra to look forward to during my summer visits home to see Mom and Dad. Now I bring my golf clubs with me and hope that we'll have at least one good day to play a round of golf.

Visits home are vacations back in time for me since some things, thankfully, just stay the same. Because I consider these visits "vacations," I usually wake up much later than my early rising parents. Rested to just the right degree, I stretch, slowly move my legs from the comfortable bed to the floor, don my robe, and walk out to the kitchen where Mom and Dad are perusing the *Bangor Daily News*. The smell of bacon frying starts my mouth watering. Hearing my approach, Dad looks up. "Good morning, Susie. Did you sleep well? Looks like a good day. Maybe we can play a round of golf. What do you think?"

I grin from ear to ear. Yes! We eat a leisurely breakfast, talk about the news gleaned from the daily paper, and eventually Dad gets up from the table, announcing that he's going downtown to get the mail and will be back by the time I get dressed. "You go get dressed," Mom offers. "I'll do up the dishes." I never take her up on her offer; instead I share the task of washing, drying, and putting the breakfast dishes away.

And I know from past experience that Dad will be a while because this daily outing isn't only about getting the mail but also involves a short drive up the Fort Road and the likely possibility of running into someone, either at the post office or the gas station, who will strike up a conversation with him. He loves this morning routine and we learn after his passing, that the many people he converses with on a regular basis truly miss him.

I'm ready before he returns. While Dad's out, Mom and I plan a shopping trip to Presque Isle later in the day after

the golf game is finished. Before long, we hear Dad drive
into the driveway, park his truck, and come into the house.
"Not much mail, Polly. Mostly junk."

"Bring it in anyway."

"Yes, dear." He walks toward the living room, giving me
a big, surreptitious grin as he replies to her command.
"You ready, Susie?"

"You bet."

"Have a good time, you two." Mom is busy sorting
through the mail, scissors at the ready to clip any coupons
deemed worth holding on to, and as she looks forward to
an hour of saving money, we leave for our much
anticipated outing.

The golf course is just a few short miles from my
parents' home and as we drive towards our destination,
Dad comments, "The crops look good this year. We've had
plenty of rain so the farmers should have a good yield. It's
not like it used to be, though. Many of the farmers have
given up. The farmers I used to work with are getting too
old to farm and there's no one to take over. And it costs so
much more now to farm, what with the huge machines and
all. Kind of sad."

The road we are on leads directly to the mountain and
as we drive along, we come alongside the course, built on
land that at one time was farmed. It stretches for some
distance along the length of the mountain. One scenic hole
includes a winding dirt path that rises high up on the front
of the mountain. In the beginning, the course was just a
nine-hole course, but it quickly expanded once it became
clear that business would be brisk. Because of the
beautiful setting and reasonable rates, the course appeals
to the many retirees in the area and also draws in visitors
from neighboring Canada.

Dad turns into the unpaved drive and parks beside the
restaurant/club house. He bought a used golf cart a couple
of years ago which he stores in a shelter just across from
the parking lot. We walk over to get the cart before
unloading our clubs from the back of his pickup truck. On
this particular day, many of the stalls are empty, signaling
that many golfers are already on the course. The prospect
of a crowded course doesn't bother either of us. We are

unlikely to run into any golfers so full of themselves that they'll be irritated by our pace. Instead, we're more than likely run into locals who will stop to talk with Dad, holding up the people coming behind us, and that is just fine. If anyone behind us seems to be in a hurry, Dad will just wave them through. We're never in any hurry to end our game. Quite the opposite. We both want this event to go on for as long as possible.

Dad has a season's membership, but we have to go into the club house to pay for my greens fee. Because I am his guest, Dad insists on paying. "This is my daughter, Susie. We want to play just nine holes today. How much will that be?" he asks the man behind the counter.

"Hi, Ed. That'll be eight dollars."

"Looks like it's pretty crowded today."

"Yup. We're having a good day, but I don't think you'll be held up."

I'm thinking that this guy obviously has never seen me play golf. It's never a matter of anyone holding us up—quite the opposite!

Score card in hand, we leave the shop, heading for the first tee. Our bags are standing, side-by-side in the back of Dad's cart. He's dressed in his usual suntans, a pastel golf shirt, and a pair of tan sneakers. No golf shoes or golf glove. He doesn't need either. And what about the clubs? He is finally in a position where he can afford to buy a matched set of name brand clubs but his Depression upbringing will not allow him such frivolity. Instead, his set is a hodgepodge of clubs, picked up at one store or another, likely each at a sale price. His most treasured possession taking up space in his bag is a gadget that allows him to retract golf balls landing in water hazards. He hates to lose a golf ball, and this gadget often allows him leave a game with more golf balls than he came with—he'll fish out lost balls from the water hazards if there's enough time between him and the players coming up behind. In this way, Dad's golf game doubles as a fishing outing.

We each take out our drivers, a ball, and a wooden tee. "Why don't you go first," he offers so I tee up, take a few practice swings, and square up. Whoosh! If I am lucky, I make contact and the white or yellow ball goes sailing straight down the fairway a few yards. "Good shot, Susie." Not really but I accept the compliment.

Now it is Dad's turn. He tees up, takes no practice swings, but just squares up, swings the club back over his shoulder, and brings it around. Off goes the ball outdistancing my ball by a mile, sailing straight as an arrow down the fairway. "Great shot, Dad."

"Not bad for an old fella, huh?"

Back and forth we go, offering compliments for every swing. My compliments for his shots are always deserved. Mine from him are the gifts of a loving father. Occasionally, I miss the ball all together and he says, "Try it again." When I hit the ball only to have it go five feet, he tells me, "Just pick that one up and toss it ahead a bit."

If he's hitting well, he keeps score for himself. I never want to know how badly I'm doing, so most of the time I never count up how many strokes it takes me to get from tee to green. Once in a great while, though, I will do fairly well on one hole and feel some confidence that maybe, just maybe, in a million years or so, I can become a half-way decent golfer.

On most of these outings, we run into people that know Dad, and there will be leisurely conversations which catch each of the parties up on how their health is, how they've survived the winter, and how their golf games have been of late. Most of the time, I, too, know the people that Dad converses with, because these are residents who've lived in the area when I was younger. They ask where I now live and what I am doing. I enjoy being pulled into these conversations.

I have to say that our favorite hole on the course is the one that goes up the front of the mountain. Dad just loves to put the accelerator all the way down and give the cart as much gas as it'll take. The engine roars, and the exhaust trails a smoky cloud behind us. Dad says, "Hang on, Susie!" and we laugh, hoping that the cart will make it up the mountain yet again. It always does, and the reward is a view that is truly spectacular, no matter the season. In the summer, the trees are lush and the potato fields are blooming. In the fall, the colors are magnificent, the golds, yellows, and rusty reds of the maples, oaks and birches are the stuff of picture postcards. On this summer day with blue skies and cotton ball white clouds, Dad looks over the panorama and pronounces, "I bet you can't find a prettier place anywhere." He's happy to be in this place that's so beautiful and so peaceful, sharing a wonderful day with his grown daughter, who's a great companion even if she's a crummy golfer.

After we finish gazing at the beauty laid out before our eyes, we get back to our game. I love this hole, not only for its beauty but for the possibility of hitting a golf ball farther than for any other hole. The elevation gives me an advantage. Unless I hit a tree, I may actually get some distance on my swing. Once we each finish our first swing, it's back in the cart and down the mountain to retrieve our balls and move them ever closer to the green.

Eventually we reach the ninth hole, and I sadly face the end of a few glorious hours spent with Dad. As he has always done since I was a child, he's made me feel special through his encouraging words and the gentle companionship that are the earmarks of our relationship. Although neither of us accomplishes a hole in one, we spend a memorable morning together having just the best of times.

I cannot know that this last game of golf with my dad, which took place in 2005, will be the last game I ever play with him, and that in October of that year, Brian will play his last game with Dad as well. When Dad and Brian play, it's a beautiful day with plentiful fall colors and just enough of a snap in the air to alert golfers that winter will come before they're ready. The smell of fall decay and the familiar smell of potatoes still being dug from the ground are evident everywhere on the course. These smells evoke a past spent working in those fields, but for today, Dad is free from work and simply enjoying a day of golf with his oldest son. They play only the 'lower nine' holes, the original part of the course that is now expanded to an eighteen-hole course. They don't keep score because they've decided that it doesn't matter. However, Dad will have a memorable performance on hole fifteen...

As they approach the green, they find both balls in good positions for a putt into the cup. Brian's ball is a greater distance from the cup than Dad's so he goes first. "Almost made it," he says and then steps away to let Dad putt. Dad steps up to his ball, putter in hand, no practice swings necessary, and taps his ball which gently disappears into the cup. "Dad! That was a really good putt! You just parred this hole!"

"I did!" Dad replies and chuckles. "That's pretty good. Guess I'll keep that score!"

They continue playing with no more pars for Dad and none at all for Brian, a satisfying outing for father and son, nonetheless.

Four years after Dad's death, we find a way to honor him by arranging for a memorial bench to be placed on the fifteenth hole of the golf course in Mars Hill. His children and grandson Matt contribute money to purchase the granite bench and Mike makes all of the arrangements for the inscription and setting of the bench on the golf course. The somber gray granite seat and back are supported by curved legs and invite golfers passing by to rest awhile and contemplate their approach to the green. Tucked behind the tee, the bench blends in beautifully with the surrounding trees and flowering plants. On the back is the inscription provided by Mike: "In Memory of Edward C. Dahlgren. Medal of Honor. From your Family. A hero, a good man, we miss you." Just like Dad: a humble inscription for a humble hero.

A book about Dad would not be complete without a section dedicated to describing his life as a husband to Pauline, or Polly as he liked to call her. When Dad dies in May of 2006, they just miss celebrating their fifty-eighth anniversary on June 12 of that year. Except for hospitalizations, and there had been many for Dad, they've spent all of these many years together. As different as two people can possibly be, common hardship and loneliness likely brought my parents together; and, as the years go by, four children likely keep them together. As children growing up, we often speculate about their relationship since they so often spark: she is fire and he is ice. Somehow or other they make the marriage work as so many couples of that generation so often did.

They share a set of common values and create a stable family for us, their children, all the while being as different as two people might be. She loves a good argument and he enjoys peace and quiet. He likes everyone and appreciates a good meal; she has opinions. She loves being in charge and he lets her be the boss. It works for them. Later in life, he develops "selective deafness." Using his hearing aids to his advantage, he can either tune up or tune out her opinions.

Mom is a rabid Democrat and an avowed feminist, although she never uses that term to describe herself. She believes in equality for women and is always a force behind me. She loves her children and grandchildren and centers her world around us. Dad, in contrast, is much more in the world. He is more comfortable with people than she is and enjoys talking with others. U.S. Senators and Maine governors know him by first name, as do the many farmers whose fields he used to check several times a season.

"For better or for worse" are words from their wedding vows that in many ways describe my parents' lives together. They have good times and bad times, sometimes agreeing and at other times agreeing to disagree on issues at hand. I believe that Dad learns early on to pick his skirmishes and battles carefully—some things just aren't important enough to argue about. On the essentials, though, they are a united front. There are never any disagreements about how they will raise their children who will be expected to be honest, responsible, and hard working.

"For richer or for poorer." In their early years together, there is certainly much more of the *'poorer'* than the *'richer.'* She clips coupons and saves stamps. They wear last year's shoes and clothes. We go on picnics instead of to restaurants. But when it comes to Christmas, they

somehow are able to magically make dreams come true. They must have saved for months in order to buy gifts for us and sacrifice giving to each other so that we can have more under the tree. In their minds, "Christmas is for children."

As the years pass, we leave home and Dad's disability income increases. They have a bit more money. When opportunities to go to Medal of Honor conventions or to Presidential inaugurals come their way, they are sometimes able to go...especially in that much of their expenses will be paid for by the Medal of Honor Society. They go to Hawaii, and Los Angeles, and see President Carter inaugurated—all opportunities for Dad to reconnect with other Medal of Honor recipients, many of whom he met back in August of 1945 in the East Room of the White House. They enjoy these trips, yet always enjoy returning home, too.

"In sickness and in health." For over fifty years, she takes care of him through many illnesses. From an emergency appendectomy not long after they are married to congestive heart failure, he will experience many hospitalizations and long recovery periods at home. She is an able nurse without the formal training, capable of taking his blood sugar levels and monitoring his medications. Her caretaking is surely a contributor to his longevity. Sometimes the caretaking comes with attitude. I can still hear her tell him, "Get up. There's nothing wrong with you. Get dressed and come out and have something to eat!" Sometimes her commands work and get him moving.! At other times, he really is sick.

She does better with physical pain than with his emotional suffering which never seems to respond to her commands. As he grows older and his depression and anxiety worsen, she becomes more and more frustrated. She has survived years of his emotional blunting and distancing, unwillingness to challenge himself with a better job and with it a higher standard of living, but these more intense symptoms of his increasing difficulty with coping with PTSD are more than she can handle. Fortunately, she knows her limits and in the 1990s convinces him to see a therapist.

As the years go by and she too develops a serious heart condition, he worries about how he'll live if death takes her from him. She, on the other hand, assures him that if she dies before him and he takes up with another woman, she'll be back to haunt him. This is our mother trying to make light of her own health problems. She has no reason to worry. Dad's a committed "one-woman man."

Despite their differences, they have enough in common to make this enduring relationship last. They have children and grandchildren, a common love for the quiet life in Northern Maine, and a long history of rising above challenges. As the years go by, they settle into a comfortable companionship that lasts until the very end.

Each has definitive roles to perform in the relationship. When my siblings and I each leave home and our few chores need re-assignment, Mom gives Dad certain tasks to perform. His job list grows to include wiping the dishes dry after every meal, a job that I performed while living at home. Mom always washes the dishes. She has a system that is not to be fooled with. Dad can assist by doing the drying but she's the one in charge, handing newly washed and rinsed dishes to him. After drying, he puts the dishes back in their places, and if he happens to forget where an item goes and stores it in the wrong cabinet, he hears about it. "Now you know that bowl doesn't go there—over in the other cabinet" are her instructions when she notices that he's misplaced a dish. I suspect he really knows where everything goes; he's simply having his fun with her by teasing her. It's a game they play.

She loves to cook and he loves her cooking, especially the omnipresent desserts. Even when he develops diabetes in his eighties, she allows him a small treat at the end of the evening meal. As he sips his ever-present cup of Red Rose tea which he drinks with a bit of milk, he asks her, "Polly, what do we have for dessert?"

"How about a small piece of apple pie?"

"Boy, that sounds good. And a bit of vanilla ice cream on the top?"

"Oh, I suppose so." She gets up from the table, takes down two small plates from the cupboard, and slices two pieces of pie. She steps over to the freezer for the ice cream, returns to the counter, scoops a dollop of vanilla ice cream out, and plops it on the top of the pie. Then she serves him. "Here you go."

"Thank you. Sure looks good." And, of course, it is good and always homemade.

When she finally loses him, she stoically keeps her own counsel. We don't see tears or lamenting but simply doing what has to be done as is her pattern. We know that she misses him. She misses the teasing and the comfort of his company. She misses the daily routines of over fifty years. She misses seeing him sitting in the chair in the breezeway, putting on his shoes, his cap, and his jacket, getting ready to head to town for the mail and a short drive up the Fort Road. She misses hearing him return in his pick-up truck and come into the house with the mail and some small bit of "news" from town.

"For better or for worse, for richer or for poorer, in sickness and in health." She misses every part of him.

In January of 2006, Dad agrees to an interview for a new edition of the Medal of Honor book. Photographer Nick Del Calzo arrives in Blaine with his equipment, intent on capturing just the right image of Dad for the section in the book about his experience in Oberhoffen, France. The picture that wins out is a black and white profile shot of Dad in our living room with his medals displayed in a case on the wall just behind his shoulder. Del Calzo captures the dignity of this aging soldier and we love the picture. Dad, though, feels the picture makes him look old! Dad next sits for hours, responding to questions from Peter Collier who will write the text for the book. The tape of that interview conducted on January 20, 2006, is one of my treasured possessions.

When I'm missing Dad the most, I watch and listen to this interview. His familiar gestures and ways of phrasing a reply comfort me. His blue eyes look directly into the camera and he recalls the experiences of his war. I wonder now about the cost of that interview. Did he suffer from dredging up the memories? Did this unspoken suffering contribute to the internal bleeding that would cause him to fall to the floor at home just a few short weeks later?

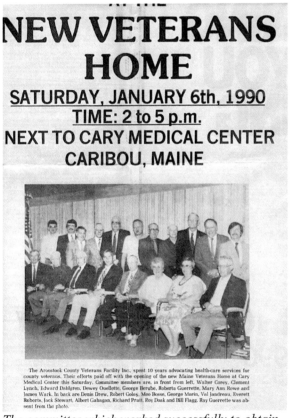

NEW VETERANS HOME
SATURDAY, JANUARY 6th, 1990
TIME: 2 to 5 p.m.
NEXT TO CARY MEDICAL CENTER
CARIBOU, MAINE

The Aroostook County Veterans Facility Inc., spent 10 years advocating health-care services for county veterans. Their efforts paid off with the opening of the new Maine Veterans Home at Cary Medical Center this Saturday. Committee members are, in front from left, Walter Corey, Clement Lynch, Edward Dahlgren, Dewey Ouellette, George Berube, Roberta Guerrette, Mary Ann Rowe and James Wark. In back are Denis Drew, Robert Goley, Meo Bosse, George Morin, Val Jandreau, Everett Roberts, Jack Stewart, Albert Gahagan, Richard Pratt, Roy Doak and Bill Flagg. Ray Guerrette was absent from the photo.

The committee which worked successfully to obtain funds to build a veteran's clinic and nursing home in Caribou, ME, pictured in January of 1990 just prior to the dedication of the nursing home.

The new Maine Veterans Home, next to Cary Medical Center, (above), will open Saturday. The bottom photo depicts on outdoor recreation area where a gazebo will be built.

Pictures of the veteran's home in Caribou, ME

Veterans home bill awaits signature

by Liz Chapman

Maine veterans scored a bureaucratic victory Wednesday, when the Legislature enacted a measure to establish state veterans homes in Aroostook and York counties. A spokesman for Governor Joseph E. Brennan said Tuesday that the bill is being reviewed by Brennan's legal staff and that chances are "very slim" that the legislation will be vetoed.

The new law, which passed without debate in both the House and Senate earlier this month, will provide for up to 60 nursing home beds in Aroostook and 120 more in the southern county. Site selection for the new facilities will be conducted by state and veterans officials, but preferred locations are believed to be Cary Medical Center in Caribou and the University of New England at Biddeford.

William J. Carney, administrator of Maine's only veterans home in Augusta, said the board of trustees will address the issue of site selection

during its regular meeting Monday. He added that "no formal action on site selection can be made until the legislation goes into effect," 90 days after the measure is signed by the governor.

"Cary (Medical Center) is a viable candidate," Carney said, "and one which we have had the most discussion with."

Funding for the Aroostook home will be obtained through conventional borrowing and also from surplus funds from the original 1977 state bond issue, Carney said. Construction of the York County home is to be funded 65 percent with Veterans Administration funds, and therefore will not be built until 1990 when VA money is available for the project.

Carney said VA funds cannot subsidize construction of an addition to an existing building, such as proposed at Cary. This fact might work in Aroostook veterans' favor, he added, because construction of the northern home will not remain "on hold" until

VA funds are available in 1990.

Albert E. "Abe" Gahagan, one of several area veterans who spearheaded the effort to gain legislative approval for the veterans homes, said "everyone is very pleased" with lawmakers' action.

"There's a lot of interest about the home. Veterans are happy that they'll be able to stay in the area for health care," Gahagan said. "That 550-mile trip (to Augusta) is a long, hard trip for veterans and their families."

The measure, sponsored by Speaker of the House John Martin, D-Eagle Lake, will affect veterans, their spouses, widows or widowers. There are about 9,500 Aroostook County veterans, and therefore, as many as 20,000 people who could be eligible for placement in the new veterans home.

Co-sponsors of the legislation were Senators Edgar E. Erwin of Oxford and Dennis L. Dutremble of York and Rep. Norman R. Paul of Stanford, all Democrats.

Newspaper clipping about the veteran's home bill

ature of Gov. Brennan

DISCUSS NORTHERN VETERANS NURSING HOME -- Veterans leaders in Aroostook County took the oportunity Saturday to speak with Governor Joseph Brennan Saturday during his short tour of the Cary Medical Center in Caribou A bill which would establish a much-needed veterans nursing home in northern Maine has been approved by both the House and Senate, but sits on the governor's desk in Augusta awaiting his signature. Pictured from left are: Governor Brennan; Ed Dahlgren, a Congressional Medal of Honor recipient from Mars Hill; and Richard Pratt, former president of the Aroostook County Veterans Medical Facility Corp Board of Directors from Bridgewater (Putnam photo)

Dad with Governor Brennan and Richard Pratt, former president of the Aroostook County Veterans Medical Facility Board of Directors on a tour of Cary Medical Center prior to the granting of funds to begin construction on the veterans nursing home in Caribou.

Ed Dahlgren, Roy Doak and Peter Miesburger, from left, members of the fundraising committee for the Maine Veterans Home under construction in Caribou, kicked off a county-wide campaign Thursday during a press conference at Yusef's in Caribou. The panel hopes to raise $105,000 for a chapel, alcove and recreation area for the veterans home. (Chapman photo)

Committee seeks donations for veterans home additions

by Liz Chapman

A county-wide fundraising campaign was launched Thursday in Caribou to solicit $105,000 for the addition of a chapel, alcove and recreation area to the Aroostook County Veterans Home now under construction at Cary Medical Center.

The fundraising committee, comprised of veterans and other area representatives, kicked off its "Making it Special" campaign at a media reception at Yusef's, with committee co-chairman Roy Doak of Caribou saying, "A lot (of donations) will come from veterans groups, but we can't raise it all by ourselves. We need the help of the private sector in Aroostook County if we are to realize our goal."

The committee needs $105,000 to complete the three construction items that were deleted from the veterans home plan last fall when the contrac-

tor bids exceeded the estimate. Doak said the first $20,000 raised will pay for the alcove, which state veterans officials agreed to reinstate in the construction plans "on faith" that the committee can raise the money.

Doak explained that the alcove must be built in conjunction with the work now underway, as it would be "almost impossible" to construct once the home is completed.

Plans for the recreation area, which includes a screened gazebo and paved walkways, along with the veterans chapel will proceed after the needed funds are raised, he added.

Members of the fundraising committee are co-chairman Doak and Peter Miesburger of Caribou, immediate past state VFW commander; Jean Harding and Milt Bailey of Presque Isle; Rev. Romeo St. Pierre of the Holy Rosary Catholic Parish in Caribou; Charles Gagnon, Clayton

Bard, Norman Plourde and Don Garron, all of Madawaska; Ed Dahlgren and Joe Shaw of Mars Hill; and Viola Cummings, Robert Mockler and retired physician Frederick Gregory, all of Caribou.

"Veterans in Aroostook County have been waiting a long time for this project," Doak told reporters Thursday. "Veterans and/or their spouses from throughout northern Maine or anywhere in the state will be eligible to use the nursing home. We are looking for financial support from businesses, individuals, civic groups and veterans organizations throughout Aroostook County."

Doak noted that veterans groups from other areas of the state are also expected to contribute to the effort.

Miesburger said he visited veterans at the VA hospital in Togus earlier this month and that many "are look-
(Continued on page 12)

Dad with other members of the fundraising committee working to raise funds for additions to the veterans nursing home in Caribou, ME.

July 3, 1986 at Loring Air Force base for the dedication of Dahlgren Hall. A proud family surrounds its hero. Dad's sister, Ruth is front right.

Dad and U.S. Senator George Mitchell share the ribbon cutting duties to officially open Dahlgren Hall.

Dad and Mom with grandchildren, Matthew E.D. Daigneault and Heather Johnston, at the entrance of Dahlgren Hall.

A retired Dad relaxing on a fishing outing in Northern Maine.

Pioneer Times photograph/Scott Mitchell Johnson
RECEIVES HONORARY DIPLOMA — School Administrative District #42 Superintendent Roger Shaw, right, presented Edward G. Dahlgren with an honorary diploma last Friday night during the graduation exercises at Central Aroostook High School in Mars Hill. Originally from Perham and now residing in Blaine, Dahlgren is one of 154 living Medal of Honor recipients in the United States and the only one in Maine. His granddaughter, Heather Johnston, was the valedictorian of the graduating class.

Central Aroostook honors graduates

Dahlgren receives honorary diploma

By Scott Mitchell Johnson
Staff Writer

MARS HILL — While there might not have been a formal commencement speaker addressing the graduating class of Central Aroostook High School Friday night, there was a distinguished guest in the audience.

Edward C. Dahlgren, originally from Perham, has strong ties to the Mars Hill community. Now residing in Blaine, Dahlgren was presented an honorary diploma for consistently demonstrating the virtues of sacrifice, perseverance, hard work, civic responsibility, family devotion and unwavering faith.

Dahlgren is one of 154 living Medal of Honor recipients in the United States and the only one in Maine.

"In the village of Oberhoffen,
(Please turn to Page Fourteen)

Dad with SAD #42 Superintendent of Schools, Roger Shaw, receiving an honorary high school diploma from Central Aroostook High School, June 8, 2001.

Dad in Togus, ME at the Veterans Administration Hospital to dedicate a plaque and plant a pine tree to honor veterans, 1976.

July 3, 1996 at Augusta, ME with Maine's other living Medal of Honor recipients to dedicate a monument honoring the 76 men throughout Maine's history who have received the Medal of Honor for heroism 'above and beyond the call of duty'. To Dad's left are Captain Everett Pope of Belgrade, US Marine Corps; Lt. Colonel Jay Zeamer of Boothbay Harbor, US Army; and Colonel Lewis Millett (back to camera; Army). This is the last picture of the four together. All have now passed on.

Chapter Eight

The Long Last Battle
February 2006 – June 2006

LATE FRAGMENT

And did you get what
You wanted from this life, even so?
I did.
And what did you want?
To call myself beloved, to feel myself
Beloved on the earth.

Raymond Carver
(25 May 1938 – 2 August 1988)

Dad collapses at home on Sunday, February 12, and
Mom first calls the ambulance service and then my sister
Judy and her husband Dale. Judy and Dale arrive before
the ambulance. When Dale talks with Dad who is still on
the floor, Dad indicates that he doesn't want to go to the
hospital. "Ed, you have to go," Dale insists. "You're
bleeding and we've got to get it stopped."

Once at the hospital, the physician on duty at the E.R.
decides to try the most non-invasive approach to
controlling Dad's bleeding. Dad is given medication and
put on watch for the remainder of the day and night. By
morning, the bleeding hasn't stopped so exploratory
surgery must be tried. Dad is prepped for the operating
room and the surgeon on duty talks with family members.
Mike is now with Mom and assures me that he will call me
once the operation is over.

I am not especially concerned about Dad's medical condition. Although he is 89, he is in relatively good health and surely the cause of his bleeding can be easily determined and fixed. However, when Mike calls that evening, there is something in his voice that tells me that I need to make the trip north. I call Brian, and we decide to drive up together early next morning.

It is a five hour drive from my house to the hospital in Presque Isle. When Brian and I arrive in Blaine, we find Mom who has just returned from the hospital. "Your dad is a tough old bird. He's gone through a lot today. If you want to go up to the hospital, I'll ride up with you."

It is only a fifteen minute drive from home to the hospital, but this afternoon the drive seems to take forever. The quiet in the car is an indication of each of our individual worries about Dad. Once at the hospital and in the room where Dad now rests, I realize it is for the best that we are all here. Tubes carrying blood and other liquids run from Dad's abdominal incision to plastic jugs attached to the wall. Dad's face is swollen so much that I hardly recognize him. "Dad. It's Susie. I'm here." I lean over his bed and put my hand on top of his. His eyes open slightly, but he doesn't speak.

"He's very sedated," Mom says. "They don't want him moving around at all."

Brian leans over and talks to Dad but still no response from Dad. We look at each other and I say, "I think we made the right decision to drive up. It might take a while for Dad to bounce back from this situation." Dad's nurse comes in and suggests that we go home for the evening since Dad needs to rest. He assures us if there is any change in Dad's condition, the hospital will call.

The next morning around eight o'clock just as we're getting ready to drive to the hospital, a doctor calls. Mom answers the phone but soon turns the phone over to me. "I don't hear so well. Maybe you should talk with the doctor." I take the phone from her and a doctor, not the one who did the surgery yesterday, tells me that Dad's condition has not improved. "We feel we have done all that we can do here. The operation yesterday didn't stop the bleeding. He needs to be airlifted to Bangor if he is to survive. I know your father has a living will, so it is up to your family to decide what to do from here." I relay the doctor's message to Brian and Mom, and we agree that we want Dad to be transported.

"How soon can that happen?" I ask the doctor.

"It will take us an hour or more to get Mr. Dahlgren ready and to arrange for the transport. You certainly have time to come up to see him off if you'd like."

"Yes, we'll do that. We'll start for the hospital now."

When we arrive at the hospital, we go into Dad's room. He still looks very bloated and is unresponsive to us. The nurses are busy getting him ready so after a short visit, we all go to the designated waiting area. In a short while, Judy and Dale arrive. Dale notices some frenetic activity down the hall near Dad's room and goes to investigate. After just a few seconds, I get up to follow him. Already Dale is returning to the waiting area.

"Susan, don't go in there. You don't want to see what's going on."

"What do you mean?"

"There's blood everywhere. They're trying to control it but Ed's bleeding out. They can't take him to Bangor."

I slump down in a chair in the waiting area and cry uncontrollably. "We're going to lose him. I'm not ready to let him go." I rock back and forth, arms wrapped tightly around my body, trying to hold myself together. For several minutes, it is just Dale and I who sit together with our thoughts and worries. Dale's feelings for Dad go as deep as the rest of us. He is in essence Dad's 'third son', the man that Mom has called on during the past several years when Dad has been sick. Regardless of the hour, and often it was in the middle of the night when Mom would call him, Dale would get dressed and drive to my parents' house to do whatever he could to manage the crisis at hand.

Mom, who left just a few minutes earlier to have a lab procedure done, returns with Brian and Dale tells them what is going on. The attending doctor comes out and says that they will have to do emergency surgery to try and stabilize Dad...otherwise he will die. The doctor will need Mom's permission for the surgery. He is straightforward with us. "Mr. Dahlgren is very weak. He's lost a lot of blood. We've already transfused him completely. We can't guarantee that he will survive the surgery." Mom wants to sign the form and I go with her to the nurse's station.

The staff working on Dad has been able to staunch the most serious bleeding, and they bring him partially out of sedation so that we can ostensibly say our goodbyes to him. We file into his room. He really isn't very aware of what is happening but we say what we have to, kiss him on his forehead and leave to return to the waiting room which will become our family enclave for the next several, tense hours.

The surgeon who will perform the operation stops by to talk with us. "You know that Mr. Dahlgren is a very sick man and that this is a very risky surgery. I want you to know that I'll do everything within my power to see him through this." He tells us that he has had experience with this type of surgery. "I served in Afghanistan prior to coming up here to Aroostook and worked on many stomach wounds. " Unlike the first surgeon who specialized in stapling and performed the previous surgery on Dad two days prior and likely missed the main problem, this doctor instills some confidence in us.

I leave the waiting room to step outside the hospital to use my cell phone to call Greg. I reach him and once again am sobbing uncontrollably. "I think we're going to lose Dad." He calmly asks me questions and promises that he'll call Matt for me and will be on his way north within a matter of minutes.

During the course of the afternoon, more family gathers in the now cramped waiting area where the hospital staff has brought juice and cookies and asks how we're doing. By the end of the afternoon, eleven of us share this tiny space and the awful task of waiting for information. Greg arrives five hours after I call him and within fifteen minutes, my Matt walks into the hospital having driven over four hours to be with us and his grandpa. Mike's daughter, Valerie, drives from UMaine, Orono, alone, skipping an important exam to be where she felt she had to be. Judy's youngest daughter, Amanda, also a student at UMaine, Orono, finds a friend who is willing to drive the three hours north to bring her to the hospital. Even Dr. Nicholas, Dad's doctor for many decades, stops by to extend his thoughts and prayers. A nurse stops by with an update. "He's doing okay. Dr. Sawyer will be finished up quite soon and will stop by."

"He made it through the surgery," Dr. Sawyer tells us. "I'm amazed at his strength. He's lost a lot of blood, but I think we've fixed the bleeding. I've left the wound open for the specialists in Bangor to close. The next few hours are obviously critical, but if he makes it through the night, we should be able to transport him in the morning. We'll be bringing him back to his room soon, and you can see him briefly. Then you'll probably want to go home and get some rest. He won't be coming out of sedation this evening."

"Thank you. Thank you so much, Doctor." Eleven echoes of thanks ring out.

Brian and I sleep fitfully at our mother's house, waiting for dawn to signal a new day. The hospital hasn't called which we take as good news. We put together a quick breakfast and sit down at the kitchen table, silently aware that Dad's seat at the table is empty.

The phone rings, and we each jump. Mom picks up and gets the update from the hospital. "He's stable, and there's been no more bleeding. We're going to prepare him for transport. If you want to come up, we'll be another hour or so before he's ready for the plane."

Mom immediately calls Judy and Mike with the news. We'll go to Presque Isle and then head south for Bangor. Because the weather is looking unsettled, Mike, who has returned home to St. David, an hour and a half north of Presque Isle, decides that he'll drive straight to Bangor to save some time.

Riverside Inn, Bangor, Maine. This three story brick building on the campus of Eastern Maine Medical Center served as quarters for nursing students for many, many decades. Now an inn serving patient's families, it's a convenient place for patients' family members to call home for a few days or weeks, whatever the case might be. We check in and find the subterranean passageway that links the inn to the hospital proper. Mom requests a wheelchair. Her arthritis and weak heart are troubling her. We wheel her through the passage with its stone and brick walls and ceilings where huge heating pipes and electrical cable are suspended. I muse silently about the many, many footsteps that have passed this way—nursing students on their way to train, families on their way to check in on loved ones. We are now part of this timeless procession, our worries likely mirroring the concerns of families from the past.

A large waiting room attached to the Intensive Care Suite is occupied by family groups, huddled together in their separate clusters. Some drink coffee, some do crossword puzzles, some chat quietly. We join this Chapel of Worried Souls and find a section where we can sit. Brian asks at the desk if Dad has arrived and the receptionist buzzes into the suite. "Yes, he arrived about thirty minutes ago. They are still getting him set up in his room. His nurse will be with you shortly."

"Hi, folks. I think we have something in common. I grew up in Fort Kent and my family still lives there." A cheery nurse speaks to us and reassures us that Dad is comfortable. "You can go in to see him, one at a time. Keep your visits brief."

As the oldest, I'm delegated to wheel Mom in for the first brief visit. "What happened?" Dad asks. He's groggy and we wonder what he remembers about the past three days.

"Dad, you had an operation. You were bleeding and the doctor fixed it. We're in Bangor at the hospital."

Again he asks, "What happened?" His nurse reassures us that this is normal for patients to ask for the same information again and again.

Mom and I go back to the waiting area so that the rest of the family can take their turns seeing Dad. I've brought my basket of knitting and take out the latest project: red mittens. Knitting is one of my stress reduction strategies, and I have lots of stress today to reduce!

"What are you making?" Mom asks.

"Mittens."

"Pretty color."

"Would you like them when I'm finished?"

"Oh, yes. I would."

The long afternoon passes and darkness comes. As the day progresses, the other family groups in the room get up and take breaks or leave for the day. Other groups come to replace the original ones. We've been told that the surgery to close the abdominal wound is scheduled for tomorrow and that Dad will be under heavy sedation for the rest of today to keep him still. There isn't any more we can do for now, so we call it a day and return to our rooms to try to rest.

The hospital cafeteria becomes our restaurant of choice. After breakfast the next morning, we head to the waiting area of intensive care to check in on Dad. We sign in, and his nurse comes out shortly.

"He had a good night. We'll be prepping him for surgery soon. You can each go in."

Dad appears about the same, no better, no worse... except that the extreme swelling in his face seems to have diminished. He must be passing fluids, and that is a good thing.

He asks again, "Where am I? What happened?" We tell him again, holding his hand and reassuring him that he's doing fine.

And then we return to the waiting room to wait some more. As per yesterday, family groups arrive, some familiar faces from yesterday and some new groups. We chat with those that are close by and find out bits and pieces of their stories: a heart attack, an accident, a negative response to cancer treatment. We all belong to the same parish—the Chapel of Worried Souls.

Lunch in the hospital cafeteria. "I think I know you folks. Aren't you Brian Dahlgren?" A dark haired gentleman in white shirt and tie stops by our table. "You don't recognize me? I'm Dana..."

"Oh, of course, Dana. How've you been? What are you doing here?"

He joins us and fills us in. "My wife just had surgery. I live in the area now. I'm selling cars and ministering to a church in Orrington."

Dana has great stories, and we welcome the chance for some laughter. Mike and Dana were in the same class in elementary school...until Dana "got held back." Dana recalls his troubles with 'Leaping Lena," the seventh grade teacher who put him in a trash barrel to teach him a lesson. "Boy, she was mean."

"Awfully good to see you folks. I'll stop in and say a prayer for Ed if that would be okay."

"Dana. Please do. Hope your wife will be home soon."

We return to wait. Eventually, the surgeon comes through the double doors. "Mr. Dahlgren did well. The surgeon in Presque Isle did an excellent job taking care of the bleeding. His stitches are holding. Your dad has been through a lot. Three surgeries in the past week. And he's how old? Eighty-nine. That's incredible. He must have a strong will to live. He'll be with us here in recovery for the next few days and then we'll move him up to one of the floors." Dana's prayers must be working.

A special visitor arrives. Dr. Eric Nicholas and his wife have made the long trip from Mars Hill and will stay at the Ronald MacDonald House for a few days. He asks if there is anything he can do for us. Mike introduces him to his daughter, Valerie, and tells the doctor how Valerie missed an important exam to be with her grandfather. Dr. Nicholas offers to write a letter to her professor, explaining her absence in detail and asking the professor to allow her to make up the test. The letter worked. If Dad had been conscious he would have been very thankful for what Dr. Nicholas had done.

We stay for several more days. We can't stay forever. Work calls. We decide among us a visitation schedule so that Dad will have company on a regular basis. Fortunately, two grandchildren live in Bangor and will be in frequently. As we pack up, check out, and prepare to head north or south, I can't remember a time when I've felt closer to my family. Without speaking the words, we've realized how much we mean to each other and how central Dad is to our world.

A full month has passed since Dad's initial surgery, and he's still hospitalized in Bangor. We all visit frequently during the month. Dad also has a special guest during his stay there. The governor of Maine, John Baldacci, stops in to see him on a weekend when he's in Bangor to visit family. Although his visit is a surprise to Dad, he is certainly comfortable through it all, this last of many times when he and Governor Baldacci have seen each other. The governor has come to see Dad at our home in Blaine; on one occasion when the two were together, he later commented to a colleague, "I just had the most enjoyable afternoon since becoming governor, having spent time with Eddie Dahlgren in Aroostook County."

On the weekend in March before his birthday, I drive up with a present and a card. Brian's there, too. Dad has been moved to a different room in the rehabilitation section of the hospital. He's alert when I enter his room. "Hi, Dad. How are you doing?"

"Not so good."

During the visit, he turns to Brian and me and says with solemn seriousness, "You know, if I can't get better, I really don't want to live. I don't want to live like this." "Like this" means dependent on others for such basic care as using the bathroom, eating, and moving from place to place. This proudly dignified man can't fathom a future such as this.

"We know, Dad. We know. But you are getting better every day. It's just going to take time."

Although we reassure him, we're concerned about his condition. He's lost weight and is having trouble with eating and digesting. He tires easily. We're afraid that he might be giving up the fight.

Two days later, on March 14th, I call and wish him a happy birthday. I've sent flowers: blue irises and yellow chrysanthemums, Sweden's colors. He has had company: Brian, Mom, Judy, and Heather have come from opposite directions. "Matt was just here," he says.

I'm concerned about his tone. Usually, our birthday talks are punctuated with laughter about getting older and such. He has no laughter for me today.

Later, I call my Matt to ask about his visit. Matt tries to hold back tears. "I don't know if I'll see Grampa again. I brought him a Red Sox cap and a Sox magazine. He just didn't seem too into the birthday thing. "

Two weeks later, Dad is transferred back home to the nursing facility in Mars Hill, just a mile from his home. He can rehab there and will be closer to Mom, friends, and other family members. Perhaps the move will give him some hope.

Brian drives north from his home in New Hampshire to see Dad and check on how he and Mom are doing. While there, he becomes very concerned about Dad's well-being. "Mom, I think Dad must have an infection. He's feverish and incoherent. I think we need to get him transported to the Emergency Room in Presque Isle."

It takes the entire evening to arrange a transport and get him checked into the hospital in Presque Isle. Just as Brian suspected, Dad had a major infection that would have killed him shortly if it hadn't been checked. Now on antibiotics and fluids, he has a chance. Mom is insistent that Dad will not be going back to the nursing home in Mars Hill. With Brian and Mike's help, she starts the process of getting him a bed at the Maine Veteran's Home in Caribou—ironically, the facility Dad was instrumental in getting built for the veterans of Aroostook County.

After several days recuperating in Presque Isle, he is stable enough to move. The Veteran's Home, we are told, will be honored to care for Dad.

In late April during my school vacation, I drive north to see Dad. I haven't seen him since March and look forward to some time with him. As I enter the veteran's facility in Caribou that is now his home, I'm not sure what to expect. As I turn the corner and enter his room, the first room on the left after the double doors, I see him in his wheel chair beside his bed. He gives me a big smile and looks up at the lovely occupational therapist who is working with him on strengthening the muscles in his arms. She tosses a ball to him, and he gently pushes it back to her. He has a wide grin on his face. He is obviously enjoying the attention of a pretty woman. In a short while, he's tired out and wants to return to bed. He's so thin, and I notice his legs which look like matchsticks and are likely not able to support him.

I am discouraged by his condition, not only the physical wasting away but also his mental alertness. This man who was so bright and who could talk about any subject in depth is having trouble staying in the moment. I sit beside his bed, and he doses off. I continue to hold his hand as he sleeps. These are just catnaps and in a few minutes, his eyes are open and he looks over at me. "How's Greg?" he asks.

The nurses are in and out of his room. I'm impressed with the care that he's receiving. One of his nurses stops by and asks how he's doing this morning, and he introduces me to her. "This is my daughter, Susie." She takes his vitals and asks if he needs anything right now. "No, I guess I'm okay." She gives him a quick kiss on the forehead and goes over to check on Owen, Dad's roommate.

"Dad, I'll be right back." I leave to see if the hospital social worker might be available. She's in her office and I introduce myself and sit down.

"I'm worried about Dad. You probably know from his records that he suffers from depression and anxiety and takes daily medication. He seems to me to be very depressed. I wanted to check to see if he's getting his medication."

"Yes, he is. We're giving him the medications that he was taking prior to being hospitalized. I'm sure he's depressed. It isn't easy being in a facility like this."

"He used to see a therapist, and it was so helpful to him."

"I've talked with your Dad. I'll make a point to stop in more often."

"Thank you. Thank you so much."

I return to visit with Dad for a while. He's still sleeping. I don't disturb him. I sit beside him and realize that I'm where I want to be. I drink in this moment, not sure of how many more of these moments I'll have with him. The next time I see my dad, it will be Memorial Day, a month later.

Mom calls Brian on Sunday evening, May 28 and passes along somber news. Dad has pneumonia. She asks Brian to call me. Brother and sister talk, both knowing without saying that this will be the end. He is too weak to fight this most recent illness; we know that we will be losing our dad. I break down crying, and we agree that we'll talk tomorrow.

I sleep hardly at all and get up very early the next day. I need to pack and want to leave as soon as possible. Brian has a number of things he has to do before he can leave so I decide to strike out on my own. Greg, concerned about how upset I am, questions my ability to drive. I assure him that I can do this.

I search my closet for something special. I am packing for a funeral and think of what Dad would call a pretty outfit. I select a couple of options, pack other essentials, and am off for another long trip north. I plan to drive nonstop, determined to arrive at the hospital in time to say goodbye to my dad.

As the miles click away, I cry intermittently and pray continuously. "Please God, let me have time to say goodbye to Dad. May he stay with us for just a while longer." At some point along the interstate, I know I have a sign from God that my prayer is heard. Off in the tall Maine pines is an American eagle sitting majestically atop his nest high in the tallest of the trees. I watch the eagle until he is out of sight and thank God for this gift. It is now Memorial Day, a special day for America's veterans, and this perfectly American symbol has told me that Dad is waiting.

A Love Story

"In Flanders Field, the poppies grow, among the crosses, row on row." Memorial Day, 2006. The poppies this day are of the paper variety, distributed by various veterans' organizations so that we will not forget those who served. As representatives of these groups drift in and out of Dad's room in the Northern Maine Veterans' Home, I remember earlier Memorial Days growing up, proudly watching Dad in our community's parade, waving a paper poppy at him as he marched by. Today, there is no marching. Dad has pneumonia and will not march again.

With family surrounding him, Dad drifts in and out of awareness. His hands are busy in a repetitive movement as if he is sewing the edges of his sheets, needle in through one side, thread over the top, and needle out. Is he back in the days when those strong hands sewed the tags on hundred-pound sacks of potatoes, tags that indicated that he had inspected the potatoes for quality and certified that they were sound for next season's seed? Because Dad can't tell us what he's thinking, we will never know for sure what his restlessness is all about.

As the afternoon wears on, Mom wears out. It has been a long day for her, a long winter of bedside watches. Her children are arriving from distances to witness the last act. A drama is writing itself, and she is not the director. Her control is slipping away and the only decision she can make today is whether to stay a while longer or go home. She leaves, and I decide to stay with Dad. Before leaving, she warns me about the dangers of moose crossing the roads and hopes that I'll be home before dark—Mom still being Mom, concerned about my safety.

I am alone with Dad, and I move into the one cushioned, high-backed chair that is standard feature in hospital rooms. I push the chair close so that I can hold Dad's hand. My smaller hand rests easily within his larger one, and he responds to my touch. He knows I am with him and I am overcome with contentment. There is nowhere else on this earth that I want to be at this moment. Oh, God, please let this time continue into timelessness...

Dad is trying to tell me something and I move even closer, struggling to understand. I can pick out several words: animals, cruelty, people. Had he witnessed some awful cruelty in his lifetime? Later I wondered if he was referring to how we treat animals better than people in that we euthanize our beloved animals when they suffer. Is he telling me about his own suffering? If so, I am powerless to provide relief. I can only continue to love him, to hold his hand, to bear witness to this last chapter.

Supper comes. Vegetable soup, milk, a tuna sandwich. "Would you like some soup, Dad?" A nod. I pull the tray over closer to his bed and sit on the edge of the bed. I scoop up a small spoonful of soup and offer it to him. He opens wide and takes the broth. He chews the pieces of carrot. I give him another spoonful and then he motions that he had had enough. He points toward the napkin on his tray, and I hold it to his mouth to receive the carrots that he's not been able to swallow. He lies back on his pillow and I move the tray away.

I settle back in my chair and again take Dad's hand, memorizing the shape and texture. Square hands, hands that could lift hundred-pound sacks of potatoes all day long and still have strength enough to sweep up the floors before quitting for the night. Hands that picked me up off the ground, knees full of gravel and bleeding, having fallen from my bike on my first try riding a two-wheeler. Hands that held my son on his baptismal day. Hands that restlessly tapped out a cadence on the kitchen table: one, two, three, four...one, two, three, four, five. Hands that fed me when I was just a baby. I recall a story that Mom has shared with me...

I sit in my highchair, my squirmy, dimpled self, anticipating a supper of strained carrots and applesauce. "Da Da Da Da" He mixes the Gerber carrots around in the bowl, teasing me. "Smile, Susie. Show me that new tooth." I smile from ear to ear, drooling out of both sides of my mouth, unable to contain my joy. Blue eyes meet blue eyes and I am in love, a love that would be one of the most profound in my life.

Then he fed me, and today I repeat the ritual. It is what I can do for him. As night covers this day, I hear the nurses making their rounds, preparing the patients for bed. When Dad's nurse comes by, she assures me that he will rest comfortably, that he'll have medication to help him sleep and to relieve pain. I kiss my Dad, ready to take my leave before the Aroostook County moose start to patrol the highways. "I love you, Dad. I'll see you in the morning. Have a good night's sleep." How many times have Dad and I offered each other this same goodnight? Simple words, our private ritual.

Reluctantly I let go of his hand. As I walk from his room, I look back once, twice, three times, saying my silent prayer. Please, God, watch over him tonight.

Memorial Day is ending. "In Flanders Fields, the poppies grow..."

("In Flanders Fields" by Col. John McCrea, May, 1915)

We spend May 31st at Dad's bedside, not knowing if he will live to see another day. He wakes but briefly throughout the day and gazes with rheumy eyes at each of us. I squeeze his hand and he weakly squeezes back. It's about all he can do. His breathing is labored and his lungs are full of watery phlegm. Nurses are in and out of the room, asking if we need anything. Sometime during the morning, the staff brings a cart in with cookies and cold juice. Dad isn't eating or drinking. This is for us as we pass the minutes and hours with him.

One of his nurses comes into his room and tells us what to expect in clear and non-medical terms. Dad is dying and will continue to experience difficulty with his breathing. She assures us that he isn't in pain. They are providing medication to take care of any discomfort. He will sleep a lot. She tells us that even when sleeping, he hears us; our hearing is the last of our senses to go. I am somewhat puzzled that she is saying this in Dad's presence, knowing that he hears this conversation. Later in the day, we know that he was listening when he asks, "Is someone going to Heaven?"

In the afternoon, while Mom stays with Dad, my brothers and I are invited to a meeting with the doctors, nurses, and the hospital social worker. We are asked if we have any questions. We know the inevitable is near. I ask "How long will he stay?" The answer comes, 'It's hard to

tell." It's a short meeting. We leave with some reading
material about the process of death and what to expect.

While we are gone, the nursing staff changes Dad's
bedding and dresses him in a soft pair of flannel pajamas. I
notice the beautiful quilt that's covering him and comment
on it. The nurse tells me that family members often donate
quilts in memory of loved ones and that this is one of those
quilts. I think of the quilt that I've made and had intended
to give Dad for Father's Day this year. I don't believe he'll
be with us for that special day, but now I have plans for
the quilt: it will come to this place to comfort another
veteran or family member. The nurse points out the basket
of books that she has left, books about death and grieving.

I wish I could remember this particular nurse's name.
She is extremely kind and tells us how honored she is to be
able to care for Dad, a Medal of Honor recipient. She asks
us what our plans are for the evening, and I say that I
intend to stay at the hospital. She tells us that there is a
suite available for family members with beds, bathroom,
and a kitchenette. Would we like to use it? As she and I
walk together down the hallway so that she can show me
the facility, she remarks, "I somehow expected that your
Dad would be a much larger man, given all his awards." I
reply, "Dad is large in spirit and is a very special man to all
of us." She knows what I am saying.

As evening comes on, Dale and Judy decide that they
will go home. They have worked all day and will have to go
to work tomorrow. It's been a long day. Dale leaves to go to
the car and Judy stays to say goodbye to Dad. Brian and
Mom leave for home and will return with night clothes and
toiletries. Mike, too, decides to go home to check on Tom,
his son, and to feed the cats.

For a short moment, it is just Judy and me in the room
with Dad. I am not leaving and Judy is saying her
goodbyes for the evening. She leans close to Dad and
gently caresses his feverish head. She kisses him on the
forehead and tells him, "It's okay, Dad. You can go when
you need to. Love you." She has tears in her eyes but is
trying not to cry. She turns to go, not knowing if Dad will
last the night, but she is ready to go. She has said her
goodbyes many times in many different ways. "Drive safely,

Judy. Try to get some rest. I'll call you if there is any change."

Dad continues to sleep, struggling to take a deep breath. The rattle is in full force. A nurse comes in and says that she will try to get some of the phlegm out. She assures me that it likely isn't bothering him, given the heavy medication that he's been given. Other patients wheel themselves in and provide me some company on this watch. I continue to sit close to Dad and to hold his hand.

Today I tell my Dad a lie, the first and last lie I ever tell him. Like Judy before me, I lean into him, still holding his hand, and whisper in his ear, "Dad, I know you are tired. It's okay for you to go. I love you and will be here with you throughout this time." I kiss his forehead and think to myself that in all honesty I am *not* ready for him to go, but as a loving daughter, I also do not want him to linger in pain.

Later in the evening, Brian and Mom return. Shortly after, Mike comes into the room. "I just had a feeling that I needed to be here. I checked on things at home and turned around to come back."

Dad has a semi-private room. Throughout all of this day, the nurses attempt to keep his roommate, Owen, occupied. Owen is wheeled out to the dining hall for his meals and spends the afternoon in the activity room. This evening, though, he is in his bed, unaware that a drama is unfolding just a few feet away. He channel-surfs from his bed, trying to find something entertaining to watch on television. As is his usual habit, he occasionally looks over to Dad's side of the room where all the visitors are located, hoping to engage someone in conversation. On other days, we talked with him, but our hearts were not big enough today to include another person in our very sad world. Not wanting him to think us rude, I tell him what's happening.

"Dad is dying."

"Oh, I didn't know." He goes back to his television. Shortly after this exchange, a nurse comes in to get him ready for bed and draws the curtain around his bed. We now have a measure of privacy.

We continue to talk amongst ourselves, mindful that Dad likely can hear us. We talk more for Dad than for any of us, wanting him to know that we are all with him. Mostly he sleeps but for short moments, he opens his eyes and stares ahead at the wall behind me. I wonder what he sees. At 9:45, Brian shouts, "Look! I think Dad's going. The color is leaving his body." Dad draws a shallow breath, and then another, and all is suddenly very, very quiet. One by one we caress his hands and his forehead. "Dad, we love you. You've been the best to us. We'll see you again, we're sure." Over and over again we keep up our refrain. It is simply unbelievable to us that he is gone.

We sit together for several minutes, not wanting to break apart. We are family and need to stay in this room, just us, together for as long as possible. "I suppose we should let one of the nurses know?" I believe it is Brian who breaks the spell. He and I go down to the nurse's station together.

We return with a nurse who tells us that we can stay as long as we want. She comforts us with her presence, reminding us that now Dad doesn't suffer. Once we are ready to leave, they will take over with the routine procedures. We are still welcome to use the family suite if we want but we know that we will return home—all of us except for Dad—to the little house in Blaine.

Before leaving, though, we need to let Judy and Dale know that Dad has died. I offer to call. Dale answers after the first ring and is not surprised, just sad beyond measure. We talk for a while and he says he wants to tell Judy himself.

Mike borrows my cell phone to call his wife, Micheline, who was at work. He told her "My father's gone" and she cried.

Next, I have to call my own little family. I call Greg first, only to receive his voice message. I leave him a short one. I know that he's likely gone to bed. And, my last and hardest call is to Matt: Matthew Edward Dahlgren Daigneault, my son who loved his Grampa so deeply. For several years now, Matt has had a special name for him. In Matt's eyes, he was "An American Treasure." Matt answers on the first ring. "Hi, hon. I have some very sad news. Grampa just died. It was very peaceful and I think pain-free at the end. Nana, Brian, and Mike and I were all with him."

I hear him take a deep breath and then, "Damn. What time was it that Grampa died?"

"It was around 9:45."

"That's really weird. At just that time, I experienced this terrible pain in my shoulder, like what it might feel like to be shot."

"I wonder if Grampa was sending you a message?"

"I wonder, too." Dad had been shot in his shoulder during the war, an injury that Matt knew about, but had never heard his grandfather talk about. I choose to believe that Dad was with Matt for that instant when Matt experienced the pain. Just a few days later, Matt will tell me about another message from his grampa.

Since we all experience such profound moments differently, I am choosing to include Mike's recalling of the night that our dad passed. In his own words:

"I left Dad's room early that evening to drive back to St. David to check on Tom and to make sure the cats were fed since Mich was at work. Once I accomplished that and was satisfied that things were okay at home, I figured I would join up with the rest of you back at the Veteran's Home in Caribou for the night. I shaved and showered and made a quick run to the little store in Frenchville to pick up something to eat later on; I hadn't eaten much of anything since that morning. I had also packed an overnight bag with a change of clothes and my toiletry kit. It was a fairly warm evening by normal standards as I headed back to Caribou. I couldn't help but notice how starlit the sky was, but off in the distance I could see flashing of what we like to call 'heat lightning'. Normally I would have had some music playing in my car, but on this night I wasn't much interested in that so I drove in the silence of my own thoughts.

"When I arrived at the Veteran's Home, I checked in with all of you in Dad's room and then took my overnight bag to the little guest quarters apartment where we believed we might all spend the night. I returned to the room where we all sat around Dad's bed and talked to him and with each of you. After some time had passed, I went outside to smoke a cigarette. Although the lights in the parking lot obscured them a bit, I could still make out the stars in the night sky. There were one or two flashes of lightning in the sky as well; an odd combination, I thought. Shortly after I returned to Dad's room, we tuned the TV to the Red Sox. Mother scolded Dad's roommate, Owen for having his own TV turned on too loud and the curtain was drawn around Owen's bed to afford us some privacy. As we all remember, Dad sat up in his bed during his passing and we all said our own versions of goodbye. I distinctly remember at the precise time he passed that a flash of that lightning illuminated his room, however briefly. In my mind then, and I still believe it now, that was proof that Dad 'went to the light'. He's in a good place."

The Wind Beneath my Wings

Oh, oh, oh, oh.
It must have been cold there in my shadow,
To never have sunlight on your face.
You were content to let me shine, that's your way.
You always walked a step behind.

So I was the one with all the glory,
While you were the one with all the strength.
A beautiful face without a name for so long.
A beautiful smile to hide the pain.

Did you ever know that you're my hero,
And everything I would like to be?
I can fly higher than an eagle,
'Cause you are the wind beneath my wings.

It might have appeared to go unnoticed,
But I've got it all here in my heart.
I want you to know I know the truth, of course I know it.
I would be nothing without you.

Did you ever know that you're my hero?
You're everything, everything I wish I could be.
Oh, and I, I could fly higher than an eagle,
'Cause you are the winds beneath my wings.

'Cause you are the wind beneath my wings.

Oh, the wind beneath my wings.
You, you, you, you are the wind beneath my wings.
Fly, fly, fly away. You let me fly so high.
Oh, you, you, you, the wind beneath my wings.
Oh, you, you, you, the wind beneath my wings.

Fly, fly, fly high against the sky,
So high I almost touch the sky.
Thank you, thank you,
Thank God for you, the wind beneath my wings.

June 1, 2006—June 4, 2006

Reluctantly leaving Dad in Caribou, Brian, Mike, Mom, and I drive back to the little house in Blaine late on the night of May 31st, knowing now that Dad will not be returning to this home where he'd lived for over fifty years. Once on the road home, not far beyond the nursing facility, we spot a lone moose, off in the field. He seemed to lift his head as we passed into the night, heading south to the house that now will be Mom's alone.

When we arrive, none of us is ready to leave the others, so we sit in the kitchen at the table where so many wonderful home-cooked meals have been shared as an intact family. We talk about what we need to do tomorrow and beyond. Too freshly wounded to cry, at least in front of each other, we stick to the topic of planning. Eventually, we part and head off to the bedrooms to try to sleep.

Once in the bedroom that was my childhood room, I cry and cry, unable to staunch my grief-driven tears, arms tucked tightly around my body as if to hold my very being together. Eventually, I fall asleep. Morning comes and I hear my brothers talking. It is time to get up and join my family. Brian is leaving to get the newspaper as I come into the kitchen.

"Can I get you some breakfast?" Mom asks.

"I think I'll just have a cup of coffee for now. Were you able to sleep?"

"A bit."

Brian returns with the day's edition of *The Bangor Daily News.* "Look at this, everyone! Dad's on the front page!" Resplendent in an L.L. Bean plaid flannel shirt, wearing the Medal of Honor on its blue ribbon around his neck, our dad's picture takes up a good portion of the front page. Headlines read, "Medal of Honor recipient dies at 90." Brian purchased several copies, one for each of us, and we each sit down, quietly reading the accompanying story. "Imagine that!" Mom exclaims. "I wonder what your dad would have thought of this?" I can hear his quiet laugh and his response, "Pretty good, huh?" Yes, Dad, this is "pretty good," for you to be remembered in this way.

Governor Baldacci, Senator Susan Collins, Blaine's town manager Chappie Clark, and Legion Commander and good friend, Phil Lawrence all gave statements for the article. Phil Lawrence recalls playing golf with Dad last October. "He was a very outgoing person and easy to get along with." Susan Collins said that "America has lost a true hero with the passing of Eddie Dahlgren." Governor Baldacci announced that flags would be flown at half-staff throughout the state on June 5th, the day of Dad's funeral. Reading these tributes is a salve on our wounded selves.

Once we finish reading the tributes to our dad, we gather again at the kitchen table, ready to make the lists of what we need to do in the coming days. Soon Steve Lunn from the funeral home calls. We set a time to meet with him in the morning. He assures us that he'll take care of all of the details. Throughout the day, as the news makes its way throughout our little community, friends and relatives stop by, laden with sweets and casseroles. Mom has an appointment with her hairdresser and leaves in the afternoon to "get beautiful."

On Friday, we meet with Steve at the funeral home. There is much to do: write an obituary, select a casket, set visiting hours, arrange for a military honor guard, etc., etc. Mom has decided that Dad should have a full military funeral with a Catholic mass, to be held at St. Mary's Catholic Church in Presque Isle. Steve assures us that he will make all of the arrangements. We just need to make him aware of our wishes.

Always organized, Mom is prepared for the meeting and brings important information detailing the medals that Dad received, a copy of his Medal of Honor citation, and a list of the many organizations he was involved with. As she shares this information with Steve, we once again beam with pride at all that our dad has done in his life. Although he didn't have money to contribute to worthy causes, he gave all that he had—his time and energy—to his beloved Aroostook County. The obituary ends with a request that in lieu of flowers, those who wish may make donations in Dad's memory to the Northern Maine Veterans' Cemetery.

We next drive to Presque Isle for an appointment with the priest, Father Morency, who will say the Mass on Monday. Prior to this meeting, we have some important shopping to do. Mom needs two outfits, one for visiting hours and another for the funeral. And, because Dad had lost so much weight during this final illness, we need to buy clothing for him. Brian and Mike go off to buy a sport coat, slacks, shirt, and tie for Dad. Mom, Judy, and I go with Mom to help her find something suitable. We select a pair of blue slacks and a matching cardigan for visiting hours. She thinks she has something at home that will be suitable for the funeral. We have enough time for Judy and me to get quick trims at the hairdresser and then it's off to meet with the priest.

A reserved and quiet man, Father Morency really doesn't know his parishioners well. He asks us about Dad's faith. We assure him that Dad was a deeply religious man. We don't tell him that he was the best Catholic among the lot of us! He asks us to select people to do the two readings, wants to know what songs we'd like, and I tell him that I will be speaking about Dad on behalf of the family.

Our next stop is the florist to order flowers for the visiting hours and funeral. Brian remembers that yellow roses are Dad's favorite and we all agree on a large arrangement. I order another selection made up of blue and yellow flowers, the colors of Sweden.

From there we go to a local restaurant for lunch and to arrange for catering for the reception to be held after the funeral. As we study the choices for the luncheon, Mom is adamant that we order enough. "We don't want to run out of food," she says firmly.

All of our tasks completed, we head for Blaine. It has been good to be busy and to be together.

Other family members begin to arrive on Saturday. Matt comes. Brian's children, Eric and Sarah, arrive. Sarah brings her young son, Andrew, who wanted to say goodbye to his great-grandfather. We consult with the funeral director on the appropriateness of a seven-year-old seeing the open casket during visiting hours and decide that Andrew will let us know what he is ready to do.

On Saturday afternoon, I take some time to be with my son, and we drive off to the Swedish settlements where Dad grew up. As we drive along the country roads, I find myself doing the same thing that my dad used to do: commenting on the health of the potato crops. There are fewer planted fields now than years ago because many of the farmers with small farms have found it no longer profitable to continue farming. Cleared fields, reclaimed by the forests, are overgrown with bushes and trees. As we drive into the rural area just west of Caribou, I look for the house that Dad's Uncle John built, the house where Dad lived with his mother Minnie and sister Ruth. I point out what I think is the house. It's been a long time, I realize, since I've seen it and memory isn't always accurate.

As we're driving through this land that had been settled by his great-grandparents, Matt tells me of a dream he had the night his grampa died. "Later on that night, I had this strange experience..." he told me. "In my dream, I was looking at a rolling potato field. It could have been anywhere in Aroostook, but it 'felt' like it was New Sweden. The potato plants were just coming into bloom and positioned to the right and left of an old-time wicker-style rocking chair were Grampa's brothers-in-arms from his division, in civilian dress. Somehow I just knew that was who these men were. They were assembled as a photographer would position a group of fifteen to twenty guys, shortest on the ends, tallest towards the middle. They were all smiling proudly towards the horizon as the empty chair began to rock. Then this brilliant light descended through the chair and there was Grampa, bright smile, being welcomed home, rocking in his chair as his buddies stood at his side. It was one of those 'I'm all right' moments and I felt comforted by the dream."

I believe with all my heart that Dad was sending a message to Matt that he had arrived safely on the other side. I believe, too, that his beloved Minnie was also welcoming him home. Remember, Minnie had just such a rocker: an old-time, wicker-style rocking chair, a chair that had been a gift to her from her young husband, a chair where she had gently rocked her baby Edward. I knew this chair. It was one of the few things of Minnie's that Dad had. For all of my childhood, it was stored in our basement. When I was first married, I asked if I could have it for our furniture-less apartment. Dad brought it up to us, but it was in terrible shape, having spent so many years in a dry but somewhat musky basement. It was too far gone to repair and when we moved to our next place, the rocker unfortunately went to the dump. All of this occurred before Matt was born. Matt never knew the story about his great-grandmother's wicker rocker.

We wind our way around the town of Caribou where the Swedish settlements are located: New Sweden, Stockholm, Perham, Colby Siding—once thriving small towns, now scaled back to just a few hardy homesteads. Still it's a beautiful and peaceful drive, and I treasure this time to be with my son. We head back to Presque Isle where we stop at a steakhouse for supper and then return to Blaine to rejoin the rest of the family

My brothers are watching a Red Sox game. I sit with them and we are comfortably quiet, drawn into the action of the game, giving us a respite from the past few emotional days. The Sox's biggest fan, our dad, is not in his favorite chair for this game. When the game ends, we retire to our bedrooms.

Sunday dawns overcast and cool. Today we have to be at the funeral home for visiting hours from two until four, and again from six to eight. We will arrive early to have a private viewing of our dad in the light blue casket that Mom selected. He will be wearing his new clothes and one of his American Legion caps will be resting across his chest.

Getting ready for this day, Mom's tried on several outfits, casting aside the navy blue slacks and sweater that we bought on Friday. She's lost weight since the beginning of this ordeal in February so all of her current things are much too big. Not a problem, I tell her. Her sewing machine is set up and I can alter most anything. She selects a number of dresses to try on, many of them with polka dots.

"I really don't like polka dots," she tells me.

"Then why did you buy several of these dresses?"

"They were on sale." This is a perfect example of Mom logic: if it's on sale, buy it.

After several attempts, she finds a dress she thinks will do. It needs some tucks and hemming so I busy myself with the project.

Our other task for the morning is to select pictures that we want to display at the funeral home. Steve has loaned us a display board for this purpose. Heather and Amanda, Judy's daughters, gather together the countless containers of pictures from recent and not so recent times. We select snapshots that show us with Dad, trying to give each person equal display time on the board. We also take several pictures from the living room: Dad shaking President Truman's hand, an older Dad in a picture from the recently published Medal of Honor book. This last picture is one that moved Dad to say, "I really don't like that picture. It makes me look old." Well, Dad, you have to admit that at 89, you're not what they call "a spring chicken." We all think it is a special picture of a distinguished gentleman.

We arrive at the funeral home: Mom, her children, their spouses and their children, one great-grandchild. Steve greets us at the door and welcomes us into the viewing room. Mom goes first and kneels in front of Dad's casket. She is calmly composed, a strong woman comforted by the support of her family. I go to Dad next, not entirely sure how I will respond to seeing him. I touch his hand which is cold and unresponsive. I kiss his forehead. I tell him I love him. My siblings follow me and then our children.

Guests start to arrive. Friends, neighbors, members of the community, co-workers, all file past Dad and stop by to offer their sympathies. Several people offer comforting words. "Your dad was so proud of all of you. He used to talk about you at the basketball games."

My husband, Greg, arrived earlier in the morning and is with me for the afternoon hours. When he leaves it is to make a reservation at a motel in Presque Isle, the one we had stayed at during our non-honeymoon some thirty years previous. When the last two hours of the wake are over, I leave for Presque Isle where I'll spend the night with Greg.

At the close of this emotional day, I wonder if I'll be able to sleep. Before crawling into bed, I hang up my suit for tomorrow and check to see that my written remarks are safe in my purse. With droll humor, Greg and I recall our night so long ago at this motel. Then, you could put a quarter into the device on the side of the bed and the bed would rock you to sleep! Although the beds have been updated since we last stayed here, the décor is much the same: nothing fancy, but it will do.

June 5, 2006

I wake early to find that Greg has been up for hours. Recently returned from a nearby convenience store, he has hot coffee waiting for me. I dress carefully. It's important that I look as good as I can...for Dad. I'm ready and leave for Blaine. Greg will stay in Presque Isle and will meet me at the church at ten.

It had showered during the night; clouds fill the sky, but it isn't raining now. There is just enough gloom in the sky to match this day when we will lay Dad to rest. As I travel down Route 1, the mountain is visible, guiding me home and I find some comfort in the familiarity of its shadow. Once in Mars Hill, at the intersection of Route 1 and 1A, I see an American flag in front of the pharmacy. Driving slowly through the main street of town, I'm moved by the parade of flags lining the street, all to honor Dad. At the post office, the flag is flying at half-staff, per order of our governor. I think that Dad would have been touched by these simple tributes.

I arrive home and announce, "Mom, the flags are flying everywhere!"

Soon Mike and Judy and their families arrive. Sarah, Erik, and Andrew follow. Mom has a gift for Andrew, Dad's only great-grandson. It's a bank, shaped like a golf bag holding a full set of clubs. It has sat on Dad's bureau for several years and is full of coins. "Andrew, here is something for you from your great-grandfather," she tells him. He quietly accepts the gift.

It's time to go to the funeral home which is just a short mile from our house. I realize that in just a few minutes, I will see Dad for the very last time before his casket is closed for the funeral. I steel myself not to cry. I will ask Dad for courage.

The military honor guard and state police escort are already at the funeral home when we arrive. They remain respectfully outside while my family visits Dad for this last time.

We take our turns kneeling in front of the casket. Again, Mom is first. When it's time, I kneel and touch my father. "Goodbye, Dad. I love you and will love you forever. You were always so special to me. Thank you for being such a wonderful dad. Help me to be strong today." I kiss him and sit back down.

We're quiet, subdued, each in our own spaces in this shared time and place. Soon, Steve, the funeral director, tells us that it is time to go. I walk by Dad again, touch his shoulder, and leave.

Brian, Mike, and I are with Mom in her car. Brian drives and I share the back seat with Mike. The military honor guard brings the closed casket to the hearse. We are ready to drive to Presque Isle. The state police car with lights flashing is first in the procession, followed by the honor guard. The hearse carrying Dad is next. We follow. The rest of the family swings in behind Mom's car and we turn onto Route 1, heading north.

As we move onto Main Street, Mom sees all the flags for the first time and is pleased. Cars pull off to the side of the road, all along our route for the fifteen-mile trip to Saint

Mary's. As we travel north, I notice that the clouds are breaking up. Maybe the sun will shine for Dad. We wonder who will be at the funeral, and Mom worries about whether we've ordered enough food for the reception.

We're close enough to Saint Mary's to see the sign in front of the church: *In Honor of Ed Dahlgren.* The procession pulls into the church parking lot where there are already many cars. I see Greg standing, waiting, and am glad. I join him.

Greg puts his arm around my shoulder. "How are you doing?"

"I'm okay," I tell him.

Steve Lunn opens the hearse and the military pallbearers take over. Dad's casket, draped in an American flag, is wheeled out of the hearse. We head for the entrance to the church where Father Morency greets us. The military guard removes the American flag, folding it according to tradition, and the flag of the Catholic church is draped over Dad's casket. Father Morency says a prayer and sprinkles holy water on the casket. We line up behind and to the strains of the organ, walk slowly down the center aisle of the church to the front.

We are so pleased to see so many people gathered at the church to help us send off our beloved dad. Many guests are in uniform: members of the Presque Isle police department and members of Homeland Security. I recognize relatives, old classmates, and others. We arrive at our seats in the front of the church.

Father Morency says the funeral mass. The two readings are done by Heather and Matt. I'm impressed with their composure during what must have been a difficult task. Communion is passed to those who wish to participate. And then, the priest says that a member of Mr. Dahlgren's family will now offer a few words. This is my cue to come to the podium and deliver the eulogy that I trust will do honor to Dad. "Please, Dad, help me to be strong. Help me to do this well...for you," I pray silently.

Once at the podium, I fix my eyes on the beautiful stained glass window at the back of the church, far above the crowd seated in front of me. I take a deep breath and I know I'm going to be okay. "First, I would like to thank all of you for being here to help us celebrate the life of this very special man, Edward Carl Dahlgren." I then begin my address:

Dear Dad: A Final Tribute to Our Dad,
Edward C. Dahlgren,
from Susan, Brian, Mike, and Judy
June 5, 2006

Dear Dad, did you ever know that you were our hero? That you were everything we would want to be? That we could fly higher than the eagles... because you were the wind beneath our wings. Thank God for you. Thank God for you. Thank God for you, the wind beneath our wings. Today, we come to this place before this crowd of people to say farewell and to thank you for being the very best of fathers.

Dear Dad, you lived your life with quiet dignity and you left us, when your time came, with the same quiet dignity. In life and in death, you were the bravest man we ever knew. You were the most humble of men, unpretentious, the genuine article, a man who never sought public acclaim but one who so deserved a nation's gratitude for "conspicuous gallantry and intrepidity involving the risk of life above and beyond the call of duty," action which earned you the right to wear the Congressional Medal of Honor, our nation's highest military award.

Dear Dad, we are grateful to God for sparing your life on the battlefields of North Africa and Europe, for watching over you as you lay wounded on a mountainside in Italy, for returning you to the fields and streams of Aroostook County where you raised a family and left behind a legacy of service to your community.

Dear Dad, we thank you for all that you taught us, for the lessons we learned about living well as we watched you live your own way. You taught us through your own example that kindness and goodness given are returned a hundredfold. You taught us that family matters most. You taught us to give every job the very best that we have to give, to get up every morning and go to work. You taught us that it is important to vote, to contribute to our communities, and to stay in school as long as possible. And, you taught us what it is to be a leader. In one of your last interviews for the updated edition of a book about Medal of Honor recipients, you spoke eloquently about leadership. In your own words, you said, "As a platoon leader, I did my very best to protect my men—with the help of God." You often told us that you never expected your men to do anything that you wouldn't do. You led by example in war and in peace. Growing up, we always felt safe, protected, when you were home.

Dear Dad, for as long as we live, we will remember you. And the twinkle in those blue eyes which meant you were getting ready to tease our mother. Our mother, whom you loved unequivocally for 58 years and whom you teased relentlessly. It was the game you two played. Despite the teasing, we always knew who was in charge. Dad, you could stare down the entire German army but a 4'10" Irish woman, our mother, ruled the roost. We think you let that happen.

Dear Dad, we remember fishing for brook trout with you and the fish we caught. Let's just say that when the fishing was good, we sometimes forgot to count just how many we caught. And we remember your reputation as a cribbage player. You rarely lost a game. We remember the time when your friend and fellow card player, Burt Taylor, beat you. Burt got so excited that he ran over to the Exxon station to tell the regulars, "You won't believe it. I just beat Eddie Dahlgren." To which the awe-struck crowd replied, "You did?" And we remember how you loved the Red Sox and the many times you'd say with disgust, "They aren't a darned bit of good," yet faithfully tune in for every game. And we remember when you took up golf, late in life, and how you loved to play against the backdrop of Mars Hill Mountain. When playing with you, the score didn't really matter, and taking a 'preferred lie' was okay, and just the time together was so much more important than the game itself.

Dear Dad, we thank you for not only loving us but also for being a loving grampa to our children and grandchildren: Matt, Sarah, Erik, Valerie, Thomas, Heather, Amanda, Andrew, and Emma. Grampa, Bubby, Great-grandfather—you were the best. And we thank you for embracing our husbands and wives and calling them your sons and daughters. From Dale, Greg, and Micheline: Thank you.

Dear Dad, we are sure going to miss you. We missed you Friday, Judy's birthday. You weren't with us to sing "Happy Birthday" or to ask "How's the birthday girl?" We're going to miss talking with you on Sunday mornings. We're going to miss picking out a Father's Day card that says just the right thing.

We'll miss your physical presence but will be sustained both by our many memories of you, and by the belief that you are still with us in spirit and will be so forever. We are comforted that perhaps these words from Shakespeare apply to you:

"And when he shall die, take him and cut him out in little stars, and he shall make the face of heaven so fine that all the world will be in love with night and pay no worship to the garish sun."

And so, dear, dear Dad, you will continue to be our hero, the wind beneath our wings. And when we are missing you most, we will turn our eyes heavenwards where the stars will remind us of the loveliness of you.

Rest well, dear Dad, All our love forever, Susan, Brian, Mike, and Judy"

I pick up my papers, walk past Dad's casket, gently touching the flag, and return to my seat. I hope that I did him justice.

The service is over and to the strains of 'God Bless America," we follow Dad down the center aisle, past the crowd that sings along, and out into the sunshine of June 5th.

As we ready to make the return trip to Mars Hill and to Pierce Cemetery where Dad will rest in peace, one of the military honor guards taps on the window next to where I'm sitting. I roll down the window and he apologizes, "I'm sorry if this is an intrusion but one of the reporters is wondering if you'd be willing to say a few words?"

Like Dad who was always polite, I know that I need to do this. "Sure."

The reporter is from one of the Portland stations and says, "First, let me offer my condolences. I was struck by the passage in your speech where you talked about "the quiet dignity" of your dad. Would you mind saying a few words about him?"

"That phrase describes him and how he lived his life. To us, he was just the most wonderful father and that's what we'll remember most about him. That and his humility. He was always quick to credit all of the soldiers who fought in the war, many who didn't return. He wondered why he got the chance to come home. We'll never know the answer to that question but are just grateful that he lived to become our father."

"Thank you so much for taking the time to talk with me."

The next leg of our journey begins. The procession is lead by the Maine state police and the Presque Isle police, who escort us as far as the border of Presque Isle and then turn off. As we drive to Pierce Cemetery, we remember how this ride was one of Dad's daily routines for so many years. He'd drive past the cemetery, checking out the potato crops and eventually turn around to head for home with the mail that Mom was waiting to go through. He and Mom had a plot already at this cemetery; their stillborn son, Edward, who was born and died in July of 1962, is buried there. Although Dad could have been buried at Arlington National

Cemetery with other veterans and Medal of Honor recipients, he wanted to be buried close to home where we would be able to visit him. As we drive the route that was so familiar to him for so many years, we're struck by the reality that this will be his last time traveling to this place that lies in the shadow of Mars Hill Mountain.

Once at the cemetery, Catholic tradition and military protocol blend to carry out the tasks at hand: folding the American flag just so and presenting it to our mother, saying the prayers for internment as Dad's casket sits beside the place where he will rest, and finally the mournful strains of the lone bugler positioned on a rise some distance away from us playing Taps. I'm numb with emotion, trying to stay composed, finding some inner core of strength that sees me through. The solemn guests pass by to offer their condolences.

Reluctantly, we must leave for the reception. It is so hard to leave our dad behind, but we don't have a choice. We're pleased that many people join us at the reception. I meet some of Dad's relatives who I didn't know and file away the thought that maybe, sometime in the future, I could talk with them more and learn more about Dad as a young man. Several make a point of mentioning that the Dahlgren reunion is this year and will be in Presque Isle in August. They hope that Dad's family will come. I also learn that Wahneta Dahlgren, one of the relatives, has done an extensive genealogy of the Dahlgren family. She lives in southern Maine. I will realize in short order that, yes, I have lost my dad, but I've also gained a whole big family of lovely people with whom I share a heritage.

Our saddest day, Dad's funeral, June 5, 2006. From left to right: Susan, Judy, Brian, and Mike.

{

Grandchildren gather after Dad's funeral. From left to right: Thomas, Erik, Andrew, Sarah, Amanda, Valerie, Matthew, and Heather.

Chapter Nine

Mourning a Loss
2006 – 2009

When I return to my home in North Berwick, what little comfort I find comes from somber talks with my husband and from writing in my journal, a plain, black, loose-leaf notebook. It is my private therapy. I can't explain why this writing that I'm doing has to be done on paper and in pencil since, for years now, I've done all of my writing on my computer. I think it has to do with the physical connection of hand to pencil to paper, the old-fashioned way of writing that comforts more than the mechanical clicking of computer keys. Regardless, it is painful stuff that I do, writing down my thoughts and feelings.

I frequently break down and sob when I write. I can't find the words to express my sorrow, how hollow I feel without Dad. I've surrounded myself with assorted items that remind me of him. Pictures, interviews that he gave, his signature on a program for an event that honored him are placed around my bedroom. Every day, I wear a silver charm bracelet, engraved with a charm that simply says "Dad" on one side and his birth and death dates on the other side.

This day, a beautiful June day, I walk out to the edge of our property to the memorial grove that Greg thoughtfully planted for me. The mountain laurel, a gift from my colleagues at work, is there. We grew up facing Mars Hill Mountain, sometimes in the shadow of the mountain when the sun was at just the right spot, so this shrub is such an appropriate gift. When I gaze at the mountain laurel, I recall looking out the kitchen window at home every morning, surmising what the day's weather might be given the color of the mountain.

The memorial grove also contains a yellow rose bush that I bought in memory of Dad. I never knew until his death that yellow roses were his favorite flower. But Brian knew and ordered that beautiful arrangement of yellow roses for Dad's funeral. I know the connection now: he fought with the 36th Infantry from Texas and his fellow soldiers loved the song, "The Yellow Rose of Texas." For them, it was their national anthem. I gaze at the rose bush in the grove and remember the song and miss him immensely.

Another of my friends brought me a lily which is also part of the memorial grove. An American flag and a section of picket fence and a copse of grey birches finish off this special place. I go here to be alone with my memories and hope for some sign that Dad knows I'm thinking about him. I've become much more spiritual with his death and want to believe in everlasting life. I want the comfort of trusting that we'll be together again.

Some might think that I simply am dreaming, but I know that Dad comes to visit me one night in late June. On this night I wake up and turn my head to my right. I have an awareness, a sense, that Dad is there. He's dressed in his blue sport coat and is looking at me. He stays for just a second and then floats through the closed bedroom door and is gone. "Dad?" No answer. He hasn't returned, but sometimes I feel a warmth and an assurance that he is with me still. I want to believe.

Dad had a profound faith and believed fully in everlasting life beyond this world. He found Catholicism in his sixties after he retired and started to suffer more intensely the pain from PTSD. Searching for reasons why he was spared in the war, he came to find some peace in the Church. He practiced his faith in many ways, serving on the parish council and giving his time to charitable activities. If I could believe as fully as he did, I would like to think that he is with his fallen buddies and friends who passed before him. And, mostly, I hope that he is with his beloved mother, Minnie, on the wicker rocking chair.

Her passing was his first experience with sorrow. His love for her was deep, and he often remarked in interviews that "she was a good mother." In one interview he mentioned that all these years later he can still recall her standing on the steps as he headed off to basic training. She was crying.

As he lived out his last day, looking beyond us and his surroundings to something that held his attention in his waking interludes, I believe that he was drawn to the light to the place where Minnie's spirit dwelt.

I missed knowing Minnie. Dad often commented that I looked like his mother. In pictures of us at a similar age, we do look hauntingly alike. With Dad gone, I am drawn to know more about his early years and the Swedish relatives that I never got to know. I regret not asking more questions while I had him with me. I thought I had more time. Was he happy? Did his life turn out the way he hoped? Did he have any regrets? I'm blessed with memories of many stories that he told, stories of growing up with the many uncles and cousins, but I hunger for even more.

This first summer without Dad moves along. With August, I find that I still suffer. I think a lot about Dad today...and yesterday...and the day before that... I can sometimes make it through whole days now without crying, but then like a sudden summer shower, my tears will start to flow. Today in early August, just writing the first sentence on this page triggers the tears. Earlier today when I visited the memorial grove in our backyard and looked at Dad's yellow rose bush, I almost didn't cry. As I sat in the lawn chair, facing the rose bush, a gentle breeze stirred the leaves on the grey birch trees. I cried then, silently asking, "Dad, are you there?" I still wonder if his spirit is close. And, as each day passes, I realize this is forever, this hollow ache.

I remember when I returned to work in June, one of my former students came to visit, a student who had experienced the death of his beloved father when he was just fifteen. As his guidance counselor, I hoped that I had been able to provide some comfort to him as he grieved and learned to live without his dad. When he visits this day, to in turn offer some words of comfort to me, he tells me that it doesn't get easier; it just gets more familiar. I accept this observation and take comfort in it because, strangely, I don't want the grief to pass. The pain I feel keeps Dad with me. I cry but that is okay. The tears and the pain remind me that I had—and still have— this deep and abiding connection with Dad, a connection that death cannot sever.

As long as I remember Dad, he lives within me. I see him now, posing for a picture on the golf course. I had my camera with me that day in the summer of 2005 and as he got ready to take a shot on the fairway, I asked him if I could take his picture. If the ear-to-ear smile that I captured on film is any indication, I think he was happy that July day a year ago, when I plopped some balls into the water hazards and he fished them out for me with his special gadget. Oh, how I loved him.

The aching loneliness intensifies with the passing of time. The numbing that comes with loss has worn away, leaving raw emotion as my constant companion. At least for now, it's harder, not easier, with the passing of time to put words on paper. My thoughts run together, appear and then scurry away, not always staying long enough to form a coherent passage on the paper.

Noises startle me. I'm absent-minded. I drive and suddenly realize that I don't know where I am. Did I go too far? Did I miss the turn? I'm a study in extremes: crippling lassitude follows frenetic activity. Some days, I sit on the sofa, quilting, drawing the needle in and out of fabric for hours, intent on creating a quilted door hanging to herald autumn. I'm lost in a mindlessness, fingers busy, mind floating.

Yesterday, I worked for six hours in the yard, six hours of hard physical labor, moving earth and stone and plants. I lost myself in the repetitive motion of breaking up sod, digging a hole in the dirt, working the soil for planting. The smell of the earth brought me back to growing up in Northern Maine, crawling in the potato fields in the fall, working the harvest. This connection with the soil runs deep within me and I take some comfort in the familiar smells and texture. I am a farmer at heart, albeit one now with a broken heart.

This evening, I watch the Red Sox. The game has being going on for hours. Finally, 10:28 p.m. Bottom of the ninth inning. The Sox trail six to eight. I've been watching intently, hoping for a miracle. David Ortiz comes to the plate. Wack! The ball sails into the stands. A three-run homerun. The Sox win. Dad would be happy tonight.

Edward C. Dahlgren
March 14, 1916 - May 31, 2006

In Memoriam
Although our memories of you keep you close
And bring smiles and tears and comfort, too
What we wouldn't give for just another day with you.
A day to simply share a meal, take a drive on country
roads, have a quiet talk
And watch the world go by together.

Sadly missed and loved for all eternity.

...All of Us

Dad in his 80's, posing for a newspaper picture, dressed in a favorite plaid shirt, adorned with his Medal of Honor.

Epilogue

Walking in His Footsteps
August, 2009

Today is August 12, 2009, and my brother Brian and I are walking down a short and narrow street in Oberhoffen, France, accompanied by Claude Kennel and Charles Walther. Mr. Kennel tells us, "Here is where your father fought. The first house was right here. It was destroyed and is now rebuilt." Rue de l'Hiver: Winter Street, one of the short cross streets connecting the two parallel major streets in Oberhoffen.

Claude Kennel, a sergeant in the French Army stationed at Camp Oberhoffen, is our willing guide. A student of history and fluent in English, Claude looks at the hand-drawn map that I've brought from the U.S., the map that is part of Dad's military file, providing evidence for the approval by a military board of generals for him to receive the Medal of Honor. The map cites the locations of the various houses and the barn where he encountered German snipers, shooting from windows all along the street.

August in Alsace is lush with blossoming petunias, overflowing the boxes that decorate bridge railings. On the outskirts of town, the fields of corn already in tassel waft in the gentle breeze. And on this street named Winter, a small dog safely behind his fence barks his acknowledgment of visitors on the street. At the end of the street, a homeowner comes into his yard, watching the activity on the street. Five pedestrians, two unknown to him, talking and pointing at a piece of paper, a young man from the village with a video camera on his shoulder, the strangers snapping pictures with digital cameras: what can this all mean? He looks but doesn't approach us, curious but not curious enough to inquire about our activities.

Charles Walther, now in his eighties and whose gait reminds us that he has likely seen hard times, walks with us. He looks and shakes his head and in French proclaims, "No more war." Earlier today, before this walk in our father's footsteps, Charles has told us about his war, a story that I had come wanting to hear so that I might know more fully the experience of war from another angle.

Brian and I also shake our heads as we think about our dad. "How did he ever survive this? There was no cover and firing from both sides of the street!" We are more amazed than ever. Charles credits his own survival to a guardian angel. We decide that there must have been a special one of those assigned to our dad on February 11, 1945.

"Here at the end of the street was all forest then. No houses. And the Germans occupied the forest which gave them perfect cover. The day your father was here, the Germans had divided the town into three sections, cutting off the platoon that your father came to rescue from the other units." Claude continues to give us details as we turn right off Winter Street and onto Rue Principale, one of the main streets in Oberhoffen. "These houses weren't here then. All fields and woods. This is where your father likely saw the German soldier running across a field." And, being the good shot that he was, Dad made sure that this soldier's gun would be forever silent.

Up ahead is the cemetery which is also featured on the map. We turn right onto the side street that parallels Winter Street. "The backyards you see now would have all been planted with vegetables during the war: cabbage, onions, potatoes. Vegetables that would keep in the cellars during the long winter of 1944-45." Here then was the "familiar smell of potatoes" that Dad recalled in the last interview he gave. I look at proof through the fenced-in yards, now green with grass, and try to imagine the rows of potatoes in bloom in August of '44, and the Alsatian women and young girls who hoed the hills and watered the cabbages, hoping that their brothers and husbands would someday return home safely. I look at Brian and shake my head. "War is a terrible thing. So much pain. So much sorrow."

We enter the well-tended cemetery. Headstones are lined up, row upon row, each preceded by a rectangular polished stone bed, giving the impression of the beloved sleeping for all eternity. On top of many of these "beds" are mementos from friends and family: pitchers of fresh flowers, small stone figurines. Instead of the grass that separates rows in American cemeteries, here is more practical crushed stone. I notice that some of the markers have German inscriptions and when I read the dates, I remember that this area has changed hands many times throughout the centuries and that the Germans buried here were not considered enemies but simply residents. Death has no nationality—it is simply death, the same for all of us.

On this day and in this place, peace reigns supreme. The sun brushes our arms with warmth and birds chirp happily overhead. We walk on dry pavement, unlike the cold wet mud that Dad churned through so many years ago. He heard unceasing machine gun fire; we hear birdsong. He was afraid, once again wondering if he would survive this day. We have nothing to fear. I think about our gentle, loving father who enjoyed a good laugh, who out of duty had to be transformed into a hardened, callous sniper, intent on annihilating the enemy. I realize that he never would have been able to return to this place. It was too horrific for him. I hope he knows, though, how much this town appreciates his actions. The citizens here will long remember, will never forget, the young soldier who simply got angry on February 11, 1944, and took care of business...above and beyond the call of duty.

Before leaving Oberhoffen on the second day of our visit, once again, Brian and I drive down Winter Street. I want to pick up a rock from the street to take back home with me. Rocks endure; the stone I hope to find could very well have been on the street that February day in 1945. Brian and I stop the car to look for stones along the paved street. How easy it would have been to select stones back in 1945 when mud prevailed instead of tar. I see what I am meant to see: a rough stone with many angles, indentations, textures, and colors—a stone that has weathered many storms. It is exactly the right stone.

Once home from France, I place the rock from Winter Street in front of the carefully folded American flag that graced Dad's casket, now displayed along with other mementos and cherished pictures on the top shelf of a bookcase in my bedroom. I softly touch the flag and talk to Dad: "I'm home, Dad. I understand more now. And I'm ever more grateful to a God who let you come home and be my dad."

Brian and I, August 12, 2009, pictured on the steps of the Town Hall in Oberhoffen, France. Claude Kennel and Mayor Frederic Schott are to my right. Former Mayor Charles Christmann, Madame Wagner, and Charles Walther are to Brian's right.

On the banks of the Moder River, overlooking the Black Forest in Germany, this is the route the soldiers of the 36th Infantry took to enter Oberhoffen in February, 1945.

The bridge, destroyed during World War II, connecting Oberhoffen and Bischwiller, today decorated with flowers. The watch tower in the distance was used by German soldiers to report American troop movements.

Looking down Rue L'Hiver, Winter Street, the street where Dad fought all day during February 12, 1945.

Still on Winter Street, peaceful today, homes rebuilt. Charles Walther reflects on the changes.

At the end of Winter Street where it intersects with Rue Principale. Claude Kennel points out that behind this house was open fields in 1945.

Behind the fence today was a garden where potatoes grew in the winter of 1945. Dad commented on 'the familiar smell of potatoes' in Oberhoffen.

Another bridge with beautiful flowers, a day full of peace and sunshine.
Our hosts, Claude Kennel and Charles Walther pose for a picture.

Lessons from Dad

"Brian, I'm awfully sorry that I don't have much to leave you." Dad looks over at Brian from his hospital bed in Bangor in March of 2006, obviously having given some thought to the possibility of not beating this latest illness. Brian looks up from the sports page of the *Bangor Daily News* that he's been reading, sets his eyes on Dad's, and replies, "Dad, you don't have to feel sorry. I have everything I need." To himself he thinks, "And, Dad, you have no idea how much you have left me and the rest of us...much more than money could ever buy."

As we adjust to life without Dad, we, his grown children, often reflect on our lives with him and how he is still such a part of our lives today. Every time I watch the Red Sox, whether they are winning or losing, I still hear him. "Good hit. Good hit." or the more ubiquitous comment, "They're not a darn bit of good. I don't know why I watch them." And, just like him, we still continue to watch, eternal optimists, just knowing in our hearts that some good is going to come of it all. He was an avid baseball fan and we learned to love the game from him. And, we learned much more. Here's a sampling:

1. *Dress up for special occasions.* Dad was a snappy dresser and we were always so proud of him when he went anywhere. The work "uniform" of khaki pants, shirt, and worn work boots, would be traded in for a sport coat, understated striped tie, and dark dress pants. For many years, the striped tie was of the clip-on variety since no one had instructed him on the fine art of tying a tie when he was growing up. Eventually, with my brothers' help, he figured it out and bought regular ties.

2. *Always, always, be honest in all that you do.* In an interview for *Yankee Magazine* (Sept., 1981), he reflected on how important honesty was to him: "I've worked with a lot of people in my life. When you can work in an area as long as I have and you can look anybody in the eye and say

I haven't cheated you, I never did anything intentionally to harm you, then I can go to bed at night as far as anything I've done in my work and I can go to sleep. At least I've got that much to say. Not as a Medal of Honor recipient, but as a man."

3. *Work never killed anybody.* I would argue that once in a blue moon an overweight, middle-aged man shoveling heavy snow has on occasion been felled by a bout of hard work but for the most part, I believe that Dad was correct. He worked hard at his job, and sometimes took on a second job to help with expenses when we were growing up. Many years during the spring when farmers were cutting seed, Dad would hire himself out in the evenings to work in the potato house, slicing potatoes for several more hours. Those were long days and nights.

4. *Don't buy what you can't afford.* As products of the Great Depression, both Mom and Dad were experts at thrift. She could stretch a roast out for several meals and make leftovers taste even better than the original dish. He loved to play cards and bet on the horses during fair season but limited himself to just a couple of dollars per outing. Given his expertise at cards, he often came home with more than he left with. They raised a huge vegetable garden which provided for us all year long: Mom canned, froze, and pickled vegetables; August in our house smelled of vinegar and mustard from all of her pickle making.

5. *Get an education.* An education is something they can't take away from you. A farm could be lost through a spouse's death or an unlucky card game. A job could go to someone else because that individual had a diploma and you didn't. These were realities of their lives and they wanted better for each of us. From the time I first started school, I recall their praise and pride for papers that I'd turn over to them. Our refrigerator was decorated with all of our papers for years and years. They involved themselves in our schooling. Both were active in the Parent-Teacher Association and Dad served on the School Board for many years. When it was time for each of us to graduate, whether from eighth grade or dental school, they were always there, proudly watching us. I wasn't to know until I started doing the research for this book how much

Dad had longed for an education for himself. From newspaper interviews when he was just back from Europe, he talked about wanted to be a civil engineer, a dream that was never realized. Although the G.I. Bill was there for him and other veterans when he returned home, PTSD was already robbing him of potential in that he was not able to visualize a future that would include college courses for a considerable length of time. He had all he could do to get through each day without falling apart. Later in life, he would tell his therapist that he would rather have a medical degree any day than the Medal of Honor.

6. *Help others.* Dad did much for his community and his county as is evidenced in the impressive listing of organizations he belonged to. But, it's the smaller, unrecognized gestures of kindness and generosity that marked his character. For example, he'd hire one of the neighborhood boys to help out with chores so that he'd have an excuse to give him some much needed money. He delivered holiday baskets to needy families. He visited the nursing home and played cribbage with residents.

7. *You catch more bees with honey than with vinegar.* Dad was a friendly person who enjoyed people. He'd greet you with a slight head nod and a "How are you today?" and when he died, people noted how much they missed seeing him.

8. *Love your family.* Although he wasn't able to verbalize his love for us, we always knew that we were special to him. He talked with his friends about our doings and our accomplishments. When we grew older and left home to make our own way in the world, he welcomed us back with open arms and a warm smile. He loved seeing us and hearing how we were doing. We were his legacy and made his survival on the battlefields of Europe meaningful.

9. *Never forget to honor the veterans who served so that you can be free.* You don't have to support the conflict—that is your right as free American citizens to let your voices of protest be heard—but you must respect those who died for your freedoms. And *vote*, especially for those who will protect and expand services to our veterans.

Remembering and Honoring our Veterans

Many soldiers who are now returning have more serious physical and emotional injuries than for any veterans from prior conflicts. Our enemies have learned how to maim with greater skill than ever before and advances in battlefield medical response have led to more and more of these critically wounded veterans living to return home. On Veterans' Day, 2010, Vice President Joe Biden gave a speech at the tomb of the Unknown Soldier in Arlington, Virginia. In his speech he noted that "more than 40,000 soldiers have been wounded in Iraq and Afghanistan, 18,000 injured so critically that they are unable to return to duty. More than 5,700 have been killed. More than 16,000 will need medical care for the rest of their lives." Many of these 16,000 are the soldiers diagnosed with PTSD and/or Traumatic Brain Injury. They can be treated but can never be cured and will require our nation's assistance for as long as they live.

And the living veterans of previous conflicts are even now, decades after their wars, experiencing new issues linked to their wars. For example, many aging Vietnam veterans are being diagnosed with diabetes, now recognized as a presumptive illness associated with exposure to the deadly chemical Agent Orange. These same veterans are also, years after the war, re-experiencing the war in full blown cases of PTSD. Our Gulf War veterans are experiencing a mysterious assortment of symptoms that researchers are trying to identify. These veterans, along with those currently deployed, will need more and more services from the Veteran's Administration medical facilities. These facilities need to be state-of-the art, the best that this country can provide, and be complete with facilities for families who travel to the bedsides of their loved ones to provide comfort and support.

We must never let a veteran wait months and months for services and get to the point of such despair that he sees suicide as the only escape for the nightmare that is now his life. As suicide rates climb and mental health services are stretched thin, we have to act fast to provide for these wounded soldiers who gave all that they had to give. A moral society provides for its veterans.

Although my dad has passed on, his struggle is as current today as it was then, taken on by the many young people who answer a call to duty and return to us not as before but forever changed by the traumatic events they have witnessed. As a grateful nation of free citizens, kept free by the efforts of our military men and women, we must all listen deeply and often to our soldiers' stories. We must stand united as citizens of this free land and say to our veterans, "Welcome home. Thank you for your service."

References

"Aging veterans and posttraumatic stress symptoms."
(2007). Washington, D.C.: National Center for PTSD.
(www.ptsd.va.gov/public/pages/ptsd-older-vets.asp).

Allen, M. (1981). "Portrait of a Hero." *Yankee Magazine,*
45(9), 192-206.

American Psychiatric Association (2000). *Diagnostic and*
statistical manual of mental disorders. (Revised 4th ed.)
Washington, D.C.

Barnes, C., Harvey, J.H. (2000). Comparison of narratives
of loss experiences of World War II and Vietnam combat
veterans (book chapter). Philadelphia: Brunner/Mazel.

Brewin, C .R., Andrews, B., & Valentine, J.D. (2000).
"Meta-analysis of risk factors for posttraumatic stress
disorder in trauma-exposed adults." *Journal of*
*Consulting Psychology,68(5),*748-766.

Chapman, L. (July 3, 1996). "Monument honors war
heroes." *Sun-Journal, 135(9),* A 1-2.

Chatterjee, S., Spiro, A., King, L., King, D. & Davison, E.
(2009). "Research on aging military veterans: Lifespan
implications of military service." *PTSD Research*
Quarterly, 20(3), 1-8.

Childers, T. (2009). *Soldier from the war returning: The*
greatest generation's troubled homecoming from World
War II. New York: Houghton Mifflin Harcourt.

Collier, P. (January 20, 2006). Interview with Edward
Dahlgren for *Medal of Honor: Portraits of Valor Beyond*
the Call of Duty. Presque Isle, Maine.

Collier, P. & Del Calzo, N. (2006). *Medal of Honor: Portraits*
of Valor Beyond the Call of Duty. New York, NY: Artisan
Books.

Connolly, K.A. (August, 1945). "Maine Congressional Medal
winner awaits Truman return." *Portland Press Herald.*

Dent, O.F., Tennant, C.C., Goulston, K.J. (1987).
"Precursors of depression in World War II veterans 40

years after the war." *Journal of Nervous and Mental Disease, 175(8),* 486-490.

Elder, G.H., Shanahan, M.J., Clipp, E.C. (1997). "Linking combat and physical health: The legacy of World War II in men's lives." *American Journal of Psychiatry, 154,* 330-336.

Flannery, G. (May 26, 1986). "Dahlgren one of few to receive Medal of Honor." *Bangor Daily News.*

Gelman, D. (1994). "Reliving the painful past." *Newsweek, 123(24).*

Guerrero, J. & Crocq, M. (1994). "Sleep disorders in the elderly: depression and post-traumatic stress disorder." *Journal of Psychosomatic Research, 38 (Supplement 1),* 141-150.

Hyer, L.A. & Stranger, E. (1997). "Interaction of posttraumatic stress disorder and major depressive disorder among older combat veterans." *Psychological Reports, 80(3),* 785-786.

Kaup, B.A., Ruskin, P.E., Nyman, G.W. (1994). "Significant life events and PTSD in elderly World War II veterans." *American Journal of Geriatric Psychiatry, 2(3),* 239-243.

Kennel, C. (2004). *Liberation D'Oberhoffen sur Moder, 16 Mars, 1945.*

Kubzansky, L.D., Koenen, K.C., Spiro, A., Vokonas, P.S. & Sparrow, D. (2007). "Prospective study of posttraumatic stress disorder symptoms and coronary heart disease in the Normative Aging Study." *Archives of General Psychiatry, 64(1),* 109-116.

Lee, K.A., Vaillant, G.E., Torrey, W.C., & Elder, G.H. (1995). "A 50-year prospective study of the psychological sequelae of World War II combat." *American Journal of Psychiatry, 152(4),* 516-522.

Lindorff, M. (2002). "After the war is over...PTSD symptoms in World War II veterans." *The Australian Journal of Disaster and Trauma Studies, 2002-2.*

Liston, M.C. (2003). "Social work practice with World War II veterans: Impact of the war experience on the life course and adjustment in late life." PhD diss., University of Denver: http://wwwlib.umi.com/dissertations/fullcit/3111618.

Lone Sentry: The Story of the 36th Infantry Division –World War II Stories Booklet. www. lone sentry.com/gi_stories_booklets/36thinfantry/index.ht m.

Lowell Thomas broadcasts story of Lt. Ed Dahlgren over NBC Network. *Bangor Daily News,* August 1, 1945.

Maine's Swedish Colony Guide. www.geocities.com/mscguide/nshist.html 200827.

MacKenzie, D. (2005). "Trauma of war hits troops years later." *New Scientist, 187(2514).*

Pommois, Etienne. (1990). *Hiver 1944-45/Les combats de la Liberation.* Societe D'Histoire et D'Archeologie Du Ried Nord.

Regel, S. & Joseph, S. (2010). *Post-traumatic Stress.* London: Oxford University Press.

Reid, W.H. & Wise, M.G. (1995). *DSM-IV Training Guide.* Philadelphia, PA: Bruner & Mazel.

Ruskin, P.E. & Talbott, J.A. (1996). *Aging and Posttraumatic Stress Disorder.* Washington, D.C.: American Psychiatric Press, Inc.

Scaer, R.C. (2001). *The Body Bears the Burden: Trauma, Dissociation, and Disease.* New York: The Haworth Press, Inc.

Schnurr, P.P. & Sprio, A. (1999). "Combat exposure, posttraumatic stress disorder symptoms, and health behaviors as predictors of self-reported physical health in older veterans." *The Journal of Nervous and Mental Disease, 187(6),* 353-359.

Schnurr, P.P., Lunney, C.A., Sengupta, A. & Spiro, A. (2005). "A longitudinal study of retirement in older male veterans." *Journal of Consulting and Clinical Psychology, 73(3),* 561-566.

Scott, M.J. & Stradling, S.G. (2006). *Counseling for Post-traumatic Stress Disorder.* Thousand Oaks, CA: Sage Publications, Inc.

Settersten, R.A. (2006). "When nations call: How wartime military service matters for the life course and aging." *Research on Aging, 28(1),* 12-36.

Sherwood, R.J., Shimel, H., Stolz, P. & Sherwood, D. (2003). "The aging veteran: Re-emergence of trauma issues." *Journal of Gerontological Social Work, 40(4),* 73-86.

Societe D'Histoire et D'Archeologie Du Ried Nord. (1990). *Hiver 1944-45: Les combats de la Liberation.*

Steinbeck, J. (1952). *East of Eden.* New York: The Viking Press.

Sund, D. (1995). "Honor bound: Medal marked Blaine man's heroics." *Bangor Daily News.* Vol. 106, No. 199.

Tick, E. (2005). *War and the Soul: Healing our Nation's Veterans from Post-traumatic Stress Disorder.* Wheaton, IL: Quest Books.

www.ptsd.va.gov. (United States Department of Veterans Affairs, National Center for PTSD).

www.texasmilitaryforcesmuseum.org/texas.htm

www.wartimepress.com/archive-article

Ward, K. (May 26-27, 2001). "Dahlgren's memorable day 'above and beyond the call of duty.'" *Bangor Daily News.*

Zeis, R.A. & Dickman, H.R. (1989). PTSD 40 years later: Incidence and person-situation correlates in former POWs. *Journal of Clinical Psychology, 45,* 80-87.

Lieutenant Edward C. Dahlgren
Military Record and Honors

Entered the US Army in March of 1943; assigned to the Texas 36th Infantry Division

Shipped to North Africa for training, August, 1943

First action in Italy; wounded on February 11, 1944 while fighting on the slope of Monte Cassino

Entered Rome with his division, June, 1944

Landed in Toulon, France, June, 1944; participated in the Rhone campaign, saw heavy fighting in the Vosges Mountains

Promoted to sergeant and platoon leader prior to the attack on Oberhoffen, February 11, 1945

Awarded the Medal of Honor for his actions on February 11, 1945

Participated in a total of five major campaigns, serving on the front lines in combat for over 300 days

Received a battlefield commission to second lieutenant, March 14, 1945

Awards Received
Congressional Medal of Honor
Silver Star
Bronze Star with oak leaf cluster
Purple Heart
Good Conduct Medal
Presidential Unit Citation
American Campaign Medal
European-African-Middle Eastern Campaign Medal
World War II Victory Medal
French Croix de Guerre
Ordre National de la Legion d'Honneur (Chevalier)

Civilian Background and Distinctions
- November, 1945, returned to Aroostook County, Maine
- Worked as a seed potato inspector for the Department of Agriculture of the State of Maine for 35+ years
- Married Pauline Mahan, June 12, 1948
- Raised four children (all college-educated): Dr. Susan Dahlgren Daigneault, Dr. Brian Dahlgren, Michael Dahlgren, Judith Dahlgren Johnston
- Life member of the American Legion, Veterans of Foreign Wars and the Disabled American Veterans; Knights of Columbus
- Served several terms as commander of the William Cousins American Legion Post in Mars Hill, Maine
- Member of the following boards: Board of Directors for School Administrative District # 42; Board of Directors of the Mars Hill and Blaine Recreational Department; Blaine Town Council; St. Joseph Parish Council; Board of Directors of the Maine Veterans Home and Clinic
- Dining hall on Loring Air Force Base in Limestone, Maine dedicated to him on July 3, 1986

PTSD Resources

1-877-927-8387 (Veteran Combat Call Center; talk with another combat vet.)

1-800-273-8255 (Veterans press '1' to chat live with a crisis counselor, 24-hour phone line.)

1-802-296-6300 (PTSD information line.)

1-800-342-9647 (Wounded Warrior Resource Center.)

1-800-342-9647; www.militaryonesource.com (Wounded Warrior Resource Center. Clearinghouse for veterans' services/resources. Call for private help, 24 hour phone line.)

1-866-966-1020; www.dcoe.health.mil/ (Defense Centers of Excellence for Psychological Trauma & Traumatic Brain Injury; extensive, free information and services for veterans and families. Phone; 24 hour phone line.)

www.lifeafterwar.org (Website for book, *Close to Home: A Soldier's Guide to Returning from War*, written by journalist Britta Reque-Dragicevic.)

www.nationalresourcedirector.gov (Another clearinghouse of resources for vets and families.)

www.ptsd.va/gov (U.S. Department of Veterans Affairs official website for PTSD resources; extensive information and online library of printed resources, including a **V.A. Facility Locator**, for finding facilities and services near you.)

Permission to Use Song Lyrics

Lili Marlene

Original German lyric by Hans Leip, Music by Norbert Schultze and English lyric by Tommie Connor. Used by permission of Edward B. Marks Music Company

The Wind Beneath My Wings (from "Beaches")

Words and music by Larry Henley and Jeff Silbar, copyright 1982 Warner House of Music and WB Gold Music Corp. All rights reserved. Used by permission of Alfred Music Publishing Co., Inc.

The Yellow Rose of Texas

Original lyrics are public domain.

Acknowledgments

A book is never born in isolation but is rather a project that demands a supportive community in order to live. I am fortunate to have had such a community as I've worked to write this tribute to my dad. I wish to thank my immediate family first. Husband Greg and our son Matthew have been stalwart supporters from the very beginning. When I announced that I wanted to write this book, Greg bought me a new laptop and purchased my ticket for my trip to Oberhoffen, France. Greg also penned the amazing title and once he shared his idea with me, I knew that I had a title that would stay. Brothers Brian and Mike and my sister Judy and her husband Dale have all shared their memories of Dad with me, helping me to create a fuller accounting of his life with us. I am forever thankful that Mom saved everything! Mom had pictures, newspaper clippings, programs from events honoring Dad and gave everything she had to this project, including her memories of 56 years with Dad. I am also grateful to Viola Harmon, Dad's first cousin who grew up in the same household, and who, like Mom, saved everything. Viola's pictures, clippings, and stories of Dad as a young boy were enlightening. My thanks go out, too, to Viola's daughter, Barbara for sharing her scrapbooks with me. I also need to extend a sincere thank you to our own Dahlgren genealogist, Wahneta Dahlgren, who shared much of her knowledge with me over a cup of hot tea and ginger cookies.

My thanks go out to the generous and gracious citizens of Oberhoffen, France who gave their time and knowledge when Brian and I visited. I am particularly grateful to Claude Kennel and Charles Walther for their many hours of conversation and for the important documents that they shared with me. I will never forget the experience of walking down Winter Street with Claude and Charles Walther, the same street where Dad fought the entrenched Germans for one horrible day in February of 1945. I came to know the full awfulness of war on that day in that place. Thanks also to Mayor Fredric Schott, Charles Christmann and Madam Wagner. I also wish to thank Etienne Pommois for sharing her research of the war years with me and for offering much of her research in translation. I returned home with a suitcase full of accounts of the war, some of the material in French, necessitating a translator. I found a willing and able translator in former colleague, Jan Hennessey, the chair of the world language department at Dover High School.

And, I wish to thank all my friends and former colleagues who have expressed interest in my project and who have given encouragement when such was needed. Thank you for listening to my updates and to my trials and tribulations. A thank you also goes to Nancy Grossman of Portsmouth who was an early editor of my manuscript. And, Allyson Gard, my editor at Sunbury Press: you made the editing experience a delight. Many thanks. Lastly, a thank you to Lawrence Knorr, my publisher, for accepting my manuscript.

Thanks go out to Dr. Stuart Wyckoff for not only helping Dad live more comfortably with PTSD but for a treasured afternoon at his home where he helped me to know more about PTSD and its impact on my father. I also wish to thank historian Tim Frank for unearthing Dad's military file and sending me a copy, complete with records of the process by which Dad's actions were reviewed in order to award him the Medal of Honor. The map of Winter Street in Oberhoffen that was part of the file I received from Tim went with me to France and was a helpful resource on the day I walked Winter Street. And, many thanks to Col. Wesley Fox, Col. Jack Jacobs, and Mel Allen for writing such laudatory statements about this book and its subject.

Without the sacrifices of our men and women in military service who give so much to protect the freedoms of this great country this book would not have been possible. I thank them all for their service and for the many who made the ultimate sacrifice, I offer my prayers to their families and friends. And, lastly, I will be forever thankful to have been blessed to grow up with my very own hero. Thank you, Dad, for always being true.

Author Biography

Susan Dahlgren Daigneault, EdD., is a retired high school guidance counselor and an instructor at the University of New Hampshire in the Counselor Education Department. She has published several articles in the professional journals in her field and has had several stories published by *Echoes*, the Northern Maine journal of rural culture. Her work has also appeared in *The Bangor Daily News, The Maine Sunday Telegram, Goose River Anthology, and Reflections,* a University of Southern Maine literary journal. This memoir about her father, Edward Dahlgren, is her first book. Susan lives in southern Maine with her husband and cats and has one son, Matthew Edward Dahlgren Daigneault.

Picture of Mom and Dad in October, 2005, in the Shadow of Mars Hill Mountain. This would be my last picture of my parents together.